Grappling with the Gray

Grappling with the Gray

An Ethical Handbook for Personal Success and Business Prosperity

Yonason Goldson

Grappling with the Gray: An Ethical Handbook for Personal Success and Business Prosperity
Copyright © Business Expert Press, LLC, 2021.

All rights reserved. No part of this publication may be reproduced, stored in a retrieval system, or transmitted in any form or by any means— electronic, mechanical, photocopy, recording, or any other except for brief quotations, not to exceed 250 words, without the prior permission of the publisher.

First published in 2021 by
Business Expert Press, LLC
222 East 46th Street, New York, NY 10017
www.businessexpertpress.com

ISBN-13: 978-1-95253-868-1 (paperback)
ISBN-13: 978-1-95253-869-8 (e-book)

Business Expert Press Business Ethics and Corporate Citizenship Collection

Collection ISSN: 2333-8806 (print)
Collection ISSN: 2333-8814 (electronic)

Cover image licensed by Ingram Image, StockPhotoSecrets.com
Cover and interior design by S4Carlisle Publishing Services Private Ltd., Chennai, India

First edition: 2021

10 9 8 7 6 5 4 3 2 1

Printed in the United States of America.

For

Rabbi Osher Reich

Who taught me to look from every angle, to investigate around every corner, and to relentlessly seek the truth wherever it may be found

Abstract

Grappling with the Gray offers a collection of case studies, real and hypothetical, intended to ignite thoughtful consideration of ethical dilemmas and provide a guided discussion of how to approach them, working inward from both sides toward a rational and equitable middle. A large portion of these cases focus on business. However, since business has become inseparable from relationships, education, society, and headline news, the book addresses these areas as well.

What was the lesson of Enron and the myriad other companies plagued by ethics scandals? Simply stated, a business culture driven by increasing profits at the expense of values is destined to fail. In contrast, companies ranked highest for ethics grow faster than companies that aren't. Work environments are more pleasant. Employees are more satisfied, engaged, loyal, passionate, and productive. Turnover costs are less. Brand image shines. Cultivating a culture of ethics is the time-tested formula for spectacular success.

The thought questions and discussions that follow each case study are intended not to advocate a particular position, but to develop the ethical mindset that makes it possible to see a larger picture, engage in civil debate, and work effectively toward consensus. Rather than attempting to rely on compliance laws, the raising of ethical awareness will ultimately create a company culture where compliance laws take care of themselves and where every employee feels empowered, appreciated, and invested in a common vision that accelerates success.

Keywords

ethics; leadership; accountability; integrity; compliance; corporate culture; company culture; ethical leadership; mindset; ethical mindset; leadership mindset; business mindset

Contents

Preface .... *xi*
Introduction .... *xxi*

Part 1   Ethical Relationships 1
The Ugly Truth 3
Be Our Guest 5
The Gift of Acceptance 7
A Bump in the Night 9
Living on the Edge 11
Who Gets the Bill? 13
It's a Sure Bet 15
No Cancellations? 18
Bliss is Ignorance 21

Part 2   Ethical Business 25
It's All in Your Mind 27
On the Wing 29
Lights Out 32
Happy Brith-day 35
Checking Out 37
A Drop in the Cup 39
State of Mind 42
Many Happy Returns? 44
Say Cheese 46
Two-Faced 48
Invisible Customers 50
No One Here but Us Chickens 52
It's All About You 56
Commuting Sentences 58
Strolling Along 60

Part 3   Ethical Education 63
Everyone Is above Average 65
Chilling Effects 67

The Grand Design 70
The Other Foot 73
Yearning to Be Free 76

Part 4 Ethical Society 79
Behind Drawer #1 81
Share the Wealth 83
By the Book? 85
Seeds of Doubt 88
The Coin of the Realm 91
Dressed to Distress 93
Pay as You Go 96
Unimpeachable Logic? 98
Boxing for Dollars 101
In the Bag 103
Unsafe at Any Speed (Part 1) 106
Unsafe at Any Speed (Part 2) 108
Snake Eyes 111
Gold diggers 113
Leap of Faith? 115
Eye-to-I 118
Virtual Dominoes 120
On Thin Ice 123
Why Vote? 126

Part 5 Ethical Headlines 129
All for One? 131
In or Out? 134
Crying Wolf? 136
Standing on Principle? 139
Paved with Good Intentions 141
Whistleblowing in the Dark? 144

Afterword *147*
Acknowledgments *155*
Recommended Readings *157*
About the Author *159*
Index *161*

Preface

As you cross the parking lot toward your car, you realize that the cashier undercharged you for your purchase. Do you head back to the store to correct the error?

You've just finished your morning coffee at work. Do you rinse out your mug and set it in the lunchroom drying rack?

Your colleagues try to draw you into their circle of gossip about the boss or a coworker. Do you try to change the subject—or do you remove yourself from the conversation?

When you reflect on your own values and behavior, do you hold yourself accountable to the same standards you expect and hope for from others?

If you answered *no* to any of these questions, you aren't a criminal. For the most part, you haven't broken the law, and you haven't actively harmed another person in any measurable way.

But are you ethical?

Sociologist Raymond Baumhart once asked businesspeople to define *ethics*. Here are some of the answers he received:

Ethics has to do with what my feelings tell me is right or wrong.
Ethics has to do with my religious beliefs.
Being ethical is doing what the law requires.
Ethics consists of the standards of behavior our society accepts.
I don't know what the word means.

If we don't know what the word means, what hope do we have of living ethical lives? Even more worrisome: If we think we know what it means to be ethical but we're wrong, are we not on course to violate the principles of ethics despite our best intentions?

Maybe it doesn't matter. When so many around us seem to care less about what's right and more about not getting caught, is being ethical worth the cost and worth the effort? Haven't we learned through experience that *no good deed goes unpunished* and *nice guys finish last*?

It often feels that way. But is that the kind of world we want to live in? Don't we want to live in a world where we don't feel we have to choose between being good and being successful?

At the outset of the great American experiment, the Founding Fathers recognized that because power corrupts, leaders cannot be trusted to act in the best interests of the people they rule.

What those exceptional visionaries understood is that no body of laws can—by itself—preserve the order essential for the survival of any governmental system. The endless cycle of rise and fall that describes the arc of human history testifies to the limited life expectancy of any political institution.

The Framers' solution, therefore, was to formalize the implicit social contract described in the writings of Thomas Hobbes, John Locke, and Jean-Jacques Rousseau. They attempted to canonize a doctrine of universal truths and thereby add the flesh of social responsibility onto the bone and sinew of legislation, breathing a soul of life into the body of the law. Their creation was the Constitution of the United States, a document not of laws per se, but of elemental legal principles and ideals that provided the context for all future laws and jurisprudence.

The Framers were men of tremendous passions and disparate views. They ferociously argued the benefits of federal power versus states' rights, of individual freedom versus communal responsibility. In the end, they arrived at a meeting of minds based upon a collective vision of the future and a fundamental agreement over core values. This was possible only because they were guided by a mutual respect for one another's humanity and good intentions.

In other words, they were directed by a mindset of ethics.

What are ethics? What is virtue? What does it mean to do good and be good?

That is a question for the ages. And the answer is far from simple.

According to *The Oxford Companion to Philosophy*, "The major problem of current moral philosophy [is] coming up with a rationally defensible theory of right and wrong."[1] In their efforts to define morality,

---

[1] T. Honderich. 1995. *The Oxford Companion to Philosophy* (Oxford: Oxford University Press), pp. 591–3, "moral philosophy, problems of."

philosophers have constructed a variety of models that fall under four broad headings, all of which attempt to avoid the inherent problems of moralizing. Each model offers a useful, but imperfect, definition of "good."[2]

Utilitarianism defines good as whatever provides the most people with the most pleasure or human well-being.[3] However, it makes no allowance for higher virtues and objective morality. Within the framework of utilitarianism, any majority is not only permitted but *obligated* to enslave, oppress, or even torture a minority for no reason other than personal benefit or amusement. The utilitarian model effectively promotes tyranny by the majority.

A more immediate problem with utilitarianism is how to quantify *pleasure* or *benefit*. Consider the opposing factors faced during the COVID-19 pandemic. On the one hand, the virus had a mortality rate estimated between 3 and 5 percent, with debilitating and sometimes lasting health consequences for many more who contracted the disease. Medical services were overwhelmed, and burial services could not properly tend to the dead. A near-total shutdown of public activities and private services seemed the only prudent response.

On the other hand, the quarantine caused extensive hardship, both economically and psychologically. Many doctors predicted even greater long-range health consequences, as those with chronic conditions were dissuaded from refilling prescriptions and from seeking proper medical monitoring. Additionally, after the quarantine would be lifted, a second, more virulent wave was predicted for the following season.

In such a situation, what constituted the *greater good*: letting the disease run its course and dealing with more pain for a shorter duration, or sheltering-in-place to minimize immediate, devastating consequences while allowing for the likelihood of extended disruption to many more lives on many different levels? A purely utilitarian approach offers little guidance where outcomes cannot be measured or accurately predicted.

---

[2]Ibid.
[3]The conflation of *pleasure* with *benefit* or *well-being* may be an even more fundamental impediment to the effectiveness of utilitarianism.

In sharp contrast, *Kantianism* defines morality according to objective evaluation and rational consistency, applying personal values to determine universal principles. Under this system, any intellectually defensible and consistently applied value or behavior falls under the umbrella of *morality*. When applied by thoughtful, sincere, intellectually mature people in moments of cool objectivity, this system offers a reasonable approach for establishing moral tenets and determining moral behavior.

Taken to extremes, however, Kantianism validates both the Marxist rejection of private property as a social evil and the Nazi extermination of peoples deemed dangerous to society, as long as each ideology is applied with consistency. Moreover, it promotes moral anarchy, since every individual becomes the arbiter of his own moral matrix. And what happens when my moral compass sets me on a collision course with yours? Kantianism offers no solution.

Intuitionism rejects the notion of universal moral truth except as demonstrated through social consequence. Murder is wrong because it deprives another of life; stealing is wrong because it deprives another of property. Through observation and evaluation, intuitionism attempts to build a composite of virtues based on self-evident moral axioms.

However, like utilitarianism, intuitionism fails to address higher values or internal character. Like Kantianism, it fails because the axioms it defines only hold for those who agree they are self-evident. Once again, if the individuals who form the collective cannot agree on the principles of collective morality, the approach provides society with little practical benefit. What's more, intuitionalism fails to address—almost by definition—the morally ambiguous situations that each of us face as we go through life. It also comes up empty in circumstances where one principle clashes with another.

The fourth model is *Virtue Ethics* which, paradoxically, concedes the impossibility of defining virtue. Rather than attempting to articulate principles of good, virtue ethics assembles examples of admirable, upright, and upstanding behavior in an effort to teach ethics through case studies, as it were. From repeated exposure to models of virtue, we naturally absorb a higher sensitivity for goodness and organically develop into more virtuous, more ethical people. The problem is the inevitable reliance on shifting social norms, which implies no absolute standard or basis of morality.

Nevertheless, we find virtue ethics appearing in the most ancient wisdom. The model was employed 3,000 years ago, when King Solomon composed his *Book of Proverbs*, offering a collection of pithy, allegorical teachings to guide us in our quest to be good. It was similarly employed by the Jewish sages nearly 1,000 years later in their reflective tract, *Ethics of Fathers*, which remains an unparalleled guide for leading a life devoted to altruistic ideals and authentic purpose.

In my own struggle to articulate a code of universal ethics, I have found in these two sources a wealth of wisdom, insight, and inspiration. The challenge has been to adapt the language of the ancients to the profoundly different circumstances of modern times. We may not have to reinvent the wheel, but we do have to make sure our wheels are properly aligned with the vehicles of contemporary thought.

Does the collected wisdom of the ages provide an operating definition of virtue or ethics? A good place to start is by tweaking the Golden Rule: In place of *do unto others as you would have them do unto you*, resolve to act toward others in the way *they would have you* act unto them. In other words, rather than evaluating my conduct toward others relative to how I wish to be treated, I should consider my responsibility to treat others according to how they deserve to be treated. I should further contemplate how best to acquire the qualities that will make it second nature for me to respect the humanity of my fellow human beings.

Sensitivity for the impact our actions have on other people lies at the heart of the formulation offered by Hillel the Elder when asked to express the totality of Torah philosophy while "standing on one foot": *What is hateful to you do not do to another.*[4] But Hillel's brief response was far more complicated than it might seem, for he appended to it one indispensable corollary: *the rest is commentary; go learn it.*

What Hillel meant was this: Only through the accumulation of ethical wisdom can we aspire to become ethical people.

---

[4]Babylonian Talmud, Shabbos 31b.

However imperfect each model of morality may be individually, perhaps we can construct a practical system for ethical decision making by constructing a synthesis of all four. To develop your own ethical mindset, adopt the following process for cultivating moral awareness:
- Evaluate the utilitarian benefit of your attitudes and actions for the community at large.
- Apply the Kantian principles you recognize from your own experience with sincerity and consistency.
- Intuit on the soundness of your subjective conclusions by observing the objective consequences that emerge from them.
- Cultivate a sensitivity for the lessons that offer themselves up daily according to the ideals of virtue ethics.

In his classic work, *Defining Moments*, Joseph Badaracco, Jr., describes how, at critical points in our lives, we all confront serious ethical dilemmas that demand us to choose between competing core values. Such moments reveal the accuracy of our moral compass, test the resilience of our moral commitment, and shape the future development of our moral character. But our decisions in those defining moments are not made in a vacuum. They are themselves the culmination of all the ethical choices, large and small, that we have made from the days of our youth right up to each decision point.

Ideally, we should make every ethical decision only after deliberation, reflection, contemplation, and, where appropriate, consultation with the genuinely wise. But sometimes we need to make decisions on the spot, with nothing to rely on except our own experience and ethical intuition. Given the intensity of such moments, how can we be sure what's right? How can we believe in ourselves and trust our ethical judgment?

Every decision we make prepares us for the next one—not so much the decision itself but the sincere effort we put into how we make that decision. Even failure in the battle to be ethical, if we have fought the battle valiantly and with integrity, strengthens us for the next battle and better prepares us to win the war.

Ethics is messy. There is no app for being ethical, no rubric or formula to ensure that we will make the right decision in response to every ethical dilemma and every ethical conflict. Ultimately, it may be less important to arrive at a definition of virtue than to apply ourselves to the relentless task of *seeking* virtue.

King David, in his passion to acquit himself as a faithful servant of the Almighty, cries out, "Examine me, O Lord, and test me; scrutinize my intellect and my heart."[5] The Hebrew word *khilyosai*, rendered in the verse as "my intellect," translates literally as "my kidneys." Where modern philosophers describe a perpetual conflict between the head and the heart, the ancients construed the same inner turmoil as a battle between the heart and the kidneys.

We're all familiar with the heart as a metaphor representing the impulses of human emotion. The heart pumps the blood, which *boils* in anger, *freezes* with terror, and turns *bad* through enmity. *Matters of the heart* are those that bypass reason and rationality to connect directly with feelings and passion.

But what do the kidneys have to do with intellect?

The kidneys function to keep the blood clean. Without their ceaseless removal of impurities from the body, our systems would become so polluted that we would quickly fall ill and expire. In the same way that kidneys filter out contaminants from the blood, cool introspection and evaluation filter out the more inflammatory urges of our emotions.

What moderates the impulses of the impetuous heart, therefore, is the calculated restraint of the rational mind. It is the intellect that keeps human beings morally healthy by screening out the toxic influences of ego, sensory gratification, and foreign ideas. Just as the pure flow of blood is critical for a sound body, pure thinking is essential for a healthy soul.

This may explain why many translators have chosen to render the word *khaliyos* not as "kidneys" but as "reins," relating to the renal system that keeps our blood clean and oxygenated so that our minds remain clear enough to rein in our passions.

However, the capacity of reason can itself be perverted if our hearts are not committed to what is good and what is true. That's why the mind needs the heart as much as the heart needs the mind. For if sound reasoning fails to rein in the longings of the heart, the cravings of desire will give

---

[5]Psalms 26:2.

free rein to the power of rationalization. When that happens, instead of holding the heart in check, the mind becomes an accomplice in destructive self-indulgence.

In the process of making ethical choices, therefore, we need to recognize the natural tension between the intellect and the emotions, between logic and intuition, between cold reason and animated passion. Only when we can broker a truce, as opposed to an alliance, between these two capricious factions can we conclude with some degree of confidence that our choices are the right choices.

With this in mind, I offer the following collection of case studies that do not present ethical models but rather ethical dilemmas. Like any discipline, whether athletics, music performance, or cooking, the attainment of ethical competence requires an investment of time and effort. Only by developing the muscles and dexterity of conscience will we achieve the moral fitness necessary to make the right decisions when confronted by situations of ethical challenge.

One practical obstacle to making ethical choices is our inability, or unwillingness, to fully consider more than one side of an issue. We refuse to examine alternative points of view, either because we're overconfident in our positions or because we're frightened by the prospect that we might have to admit being wrong.

But aren't we better off discovering that we've been wrong, so that we can start to be right?

When we face conflict with others, defensiveness prods us to dig into our preconceived notions and comfortable ideologies. We denounce competing views as misinformed or mistaken; we condemn those who hold them as extremists and fanatics. We become more entrenched in our positions and grow increasingly antagonistic toward those who don't agree with us. We retreat into enclaves of ideology and groupthink, growing ever more calcified in our views and ever more intolerant of anyone who thinks differently.

The ethical situations presented in this book are not necessarily meant to be solved. They are meant to be pondered, debated, and chewed over. They are meant to provide an ethical workout for the mind and the conscience. As such, they will provide the greatest benefit when studied in the company of others—preferably others who don't share all our points of view.

As a final warning, it is critical to dispel the notion that what's *ethical* is synonymous with what's *legal*. If we want to be ethical, we have to buy into the truism that the challenges of ethics arise predominantly in the murky gray areas—either those that reside amidst legal ambiguity or those that we create in the nether regions of our minds. Only then will we have a fighting chance to become ethical by learning how to grapple with the gray.

Introduction

Seven Principles for Reclaiming Rationalism in An Age of Acrimony

Everyone is entitled to his own opinion, but not his own facts.
—Daniel Patrick Moynihan

I. The Steep Road Ahead

- How do members of a pluralistic, largely secular culture reach consensus on common values?
- What happens to the foundation on which civil society endures when universal truths cease to be self-evident?
- How can we the people, as ideologically diverse as we have become, articulate any ethical imperative for accepting a social contract defined not by laws but by collective ideals?
- How does it make sense to invoke a moral compass that may point in different directions for different groups and individuals?

Before attempting to answer those questions, we must first address these:

- What are ethics?
- What is morality?
- Is there a difference between the two?

II. Intellectual Integrity

Consider one of the most contentious legal debates in modern America: preserving gun-ownership rights versus protecting public safety through gun control.[6]

In the Second Amendment to the Constitution, the Framers established the canon of private gun ownership as follows: *A well-regulated Militia, being necessary to the security of a free State, the right of the people to keep and bear Arms, shall not be infringed.*

Doubtless, the authors believed they were being clear and straightforward. Two-and-a-half centuries later, determining the intention behind their words is anything but simple.

Ambiguity arises from the first clause. Why did the authors hinge gun rights on the need for a *militia*? Did they mean that gun ownership should be protected only in times of citizen armies, when every able-bodied person might be called out at a moment's notice to defend his (or her) homeland, but not necessarily when the nation is protected by a professional, standing army?

Or did they mean that defending the nation is a responsibility incumbent upon every citizen, regardless of how the machinery of warfare or the structure of the military might evolve?

Both interpretations can be defended from a position of logic and principle. Lacking the availability of a time machine, how are we to correctly interpret the Framers' intentions?

Observation #1: In fact, we have such a time machine. An investigation of writings and records from the constitutional era might reveal the general attitude toward the right to bear arms and determine where popular predisposition resided when the Second Amendment was originally articulated.

That discussion lies beyond the scope of this work. It does, however, bring us to our first principle of ethics.

Ethical Principle #1: *Discounting available information that might support one side of an issue or the other, no less than cherry-picking facts or skewing data, is intellectually dishonest.*

---

[6]Setting aside, for the moment, the claim by gun rights advocates that gun ownership does in fact promote public safety.

Political scientists have a name for the conscious choice to overlook or devalue information deemed not worth the cost of its acquisition—*rational ignorance*. On a personal level, that cost might be the anxiety or insecurity caused by knowledge that challenges our opinions or threatens our worldview.

But let's say we overcome our insecurities and do investigate; and let's say that both interpretations turn out to be equally defensible. What happens then? The next level of observation requires an assessment of the logical arguments offered by each side. Regarding the gun control debate those include the following:

Observation #2a: Gun laws already exist. The prohibition against private citizens owning automatic rifles (*aka* machine guns) has gone largely uncontested. Consequently, if gun rights advocates object to a ban on semi-automatic "assault rifles," they need to articulate why the same concern for public safety applied to the former cannot be applied to the latter. True, machine gun firing capability is much faster than that of a semi-automatic. But that is a quantitative, not a qualitative difference. How does that distinction translate into a constitutional principle? Simply invoking the Second Amendment as basis for rejecting a second exception does nothing to advance the debate.

Observation #2b: Statistically, less than one-fifth of violent gun crimes are committed with legally owned guns.[7] Consequently, while it is reasonable to argue that new laws might help curb 20 percent of gun violence, how will gun control laws have a meaningful impact on the other 80 percent? Proponents of gun control laws need to answer that question to credibly claim that their goal is ending violent crime.

Now, take a breath.

Do you feel inclined to stop reading? Do you feel anger or indignation rising within you in response to a point of view contrary to your own? If so, kindly review the previous two observations and note that no position has been presented or endorsed in either. Nothing more has been put forward than two questions, each merely addressing the *possibility* of logical inconsistency.

---

[7] A. Fabio, J. Duell, K. Creppage, K. O'Donnell, and R. Laporte. 2016. "Gaps Continue in Firearm Surveillance: Evidence from a Large U.S. City Bureau of Police." *Social Medicine* 10, no. 1.

Ethical Principle #2: *Facts and logic evaluated under the influence of emotion and personal bias invariably lead to supporting unsupportable positions as credible and dismissing reasonable positions as unsound.*

Our purpose here is not to resolve—nor even debate—the matter of gun control. But when confronting any issue, each of us has an ethical obligation to evaluate his or her own intellectual integrity. What does it say about our commitment to truth if we condemn fallacies in the arguments of our ideological opponents while overlooking them in the arguments of our allies—or ourselves?

If we are unwilling to critique both sides of any issue with equal syllogistic rigor, we threaten the survival of civil society. Why? Because such unwillingness characterizes *groupthink*, the ideological tribalism that convinces us that every rational person believes exactly as we do, and that everyone else is either misguided, delusional, or evil.

What determines whether a society is civilized and ethical? It is this: the expectation that individuals holding disparate views will practice civil discourse in pursuit of finding common ground and achieving consensus. A community endures only when its members collaborate to implement common sense, compromise on solutions that neither side may find entirely agreeable, but which all sides can learn to live with.

Ethical Principle #3: *Only through constructive disagreement and logical consistency is it possible to build a community guided by ethical axioms and committed to ethical values.*

III. Legislating Ethics

The same challenges we confront concerning political and social issues exist in the business world. One of the most dangerous delusions we face is the belief that we can prevent financial malfeasance by legislating compliance laws.

Such celebrated scandals as Wells Fargo, Novartis, Uber—and, of course, Enron—were perpetrated by individuals and organizations that flouted existing laws. Additional regulations would have made no difference.

Even worse, overregulation stifles productivity while creating new loopholes. Ambiguous wording and impenetrable language produce gray zones, while new laws often contradict preexisting ones. The more complicated regulation gets, the easier laws become to manipulate or circumvent.

But these are not the worst unintended consequences of overregulation. This is: *Attempting to legislate ethics undermines ethics.* By conflating *morality* with *legality*, we compromise the integrity of both, because commitment to upholding the letter of the law depends on respect for the spirit of the law.

Which brings us back to our question concerning morality versus ethics. Drawing a distinction between the two will prove not only beneficial but essential.

The word *ethics* derives from the Greek *ethos*, meaning *personal disposition*, from which emerges the concept of *character*. Character is the hallmark of integrity. A person of integrity is one who demonstrates intellectual and ethical consistency, who aspires to virtuous ideals, who treats his fellow human beings and, indeed, all creatures, with a fair measure of deference and respect.

The word *morality* derives from the Latin *moralis*, perhaps coined by Cicero as a translation of the Greek *ethikos*. This suggests no significant difference between the terms. However, the contemporary derivative *moralizing*, used often as a pejorative, suggests the following distinction:

Morality refers to a set of values handed down from a Higher Authority. This raises the immediate problem that a heterogeneous society will lack consensus on what that authority is, how its mandates are to be understood, and through what mechanism they should be legislated and enforced. Morality serves to guide only those who have a clear vision and understanding of the source and method of dissemination from which moral imperatives descend. Within a culture that includes a panoply of beliefs, the application of morality remains subjective and abstract.

Ethics, on the other hand, may be defined not as descending from on high but as arising organically from a set of common values. Of course, the problem remains: Without a universally recognized authority, how can there be any universal values at all?

This is precisely the question taken up by Immanuel Kant in the 18th century. As we have already explained, his principle of universalizing individual moral intuitions by applying them to society as a whole does not offer a practical solution. It does, however, provide a useful starting point.

Sincere reflection on the correctness of your actions—how they affect both the individuals around you and the society in which you live—inevitably increases empathy, thereby laying the foundation on which ethical awareness stands. A lack of empathy results in diffusion of responsibility, otherwise known as herd mentality. *If everyone else does it, why shouldn't I? If no one else is doing it, why should the burden fall on me?*

As one satirical poster observes: *No raindrop believes it is responsible for the flood.*

Conversely, the ethical citizen contemplates: What would the world be like if everyone acted like me?

Society is made up of individuals. The more responsible one person acts, the more others will feel obligated to act responsibly themselves. The more selfish or thoughtless one person acts, the more those behaviors become the norm. That's why, despite its flaws and limitations, the utilitarian approach is not entirely without merit. Attempting to calculate and quantify which course of action will produce the greater good is essential in making ethical decisions.

But it's not enough. Obvious choices between good and evil or right and wrong are not where ethics is most needed. Choosing between competing levels of evil or contradictory applications of good—this is the realm where the application of ethics is indispensable.[8]

Consequently, it is by balancing the intellectual assessment of the utilitarian against the intuition of the Kantian that we can reach acceptable compromise. As we saw earlier, the head and the heart must be brought into harmony or, at least, détente.

Ethical Principle #4*: Ethical actions are not based solely on legality. They are achieved through the application of understanding and empathy.*

Only by understanding the views and attitudes of others will we be able to relate to those who share our world. Only by relating to others will we be able to empathize and thereby appreciate the impact our words and actions will have on them.

Ethical Principle #5*: Ethics requires an awareness of both the short-term and long-term impact our behavior will have on the lives, livelihoods,*

---

[8]See J.L. Badaracco. 1997. *Defining Moments* (Boston, MA: Harvard Business School Press).

and feelings of those around us and on the society in which we live, followed by the consistent translation of that awareness into action.

IV. The Inertia of Self-Interest

Ethics is a mindset, a cultural orientation, an ideal, and an aspiration. By definition, ethics governs the vast gray area between what's legal and what's illegal.[9] The only way to ensure ethical conduct is to establish ethical idealism as an integral part of personal and professional culture.

In a perfect world, we would commit ourselves to living ethically because doing the right thing is the right thing to do. Unfortunately, the world is not perfect, and neither are we.

Nevertheless, ethics does *not* call on us to embrace altruism at the expense of personal security or prosperity. Just the opposite—it offers a way for us to have both. So how do we resolve the apparent contradiction between selfishness and selflessness? According to Rabbi Yisroel Meir Kagan, the revered leader of 19th-century European Jewry:

"We don't need to be pious; we need to be smart." If we're smart, we'll recognize that acting ethically is in our own best interest.

Ethical Principle #6: *We don't need to choose between being good and being successful. What is best for us is to live in a world we make better by promoting ethical values and modeling ethical behavior.*

Contemplate the ways you measurably benefit yourself through ethical actions. Calculate how often unethical behavior leads to self-destruction. Reflection on both provides a powerful incentive for making ethical choices.

Of course, this is easier said than done. Consider the numerous hot-button issues tearing our communities apart: gun control, abortion, climate change, hate speech, wealth distribution, affirmative action. All these skirmishes in the contemporary culture war create the impression of a house divided violently against itself, a society on the brink of collapse. And perception rapidly becomes reality.

Emotions run so high that the mere mention of social or political ideology shuts down rational discourse and renders impossible the hope

---

[9] For purposes of this discussion, we will leave aside the complex discussion of addressing immoral or unethical laws.

of amicable compromise. But there is one thing that all of us can agree on: We want to make more money. And the way to make more money is not by treating other people like products or resources, but by treating them like partners.

According to research by the Trust Edge Leadership Institute, employees say what they want most from a job is an employer they trust. What creates trust? Ethical leadership.[10]

Everything else follows naturally. Ethics creates trust. Trust promotes loyalty. Loyalty generates passion. Passion drives productivity. Employees who feel part of a team and take pride in its mission are happy employees. Happy employees are the key to prosperity, profitability, and success according to virtually every metric.

Over half-a-trillion dollars in productivity are estimated lost each year in the U.S. due to workplace disengagement and conflict.[11] For every discontented employee who leaves for greener pastures, the resulting costs of hiring, onboarding, training, ramp time, higher business error rates, and general loss of engagement are estimated as high as 213 percent of their annual salary.[12] And that doesn't even account for the toxic impact high turnover has on workplace environment and company culture.[13]

It also doesn't account for damage to brand image, which can crash overnight from blunders and scandals that an ethical mindset could have forestalled. United Airlines, Expedia, and Memorial Sloan Kettering are just a few recent examples having seen brand collapse follow ethics scandals.

That's why *good ethics is good business.* Companies ranked highest for ethics outperformed the Russell 1000 index throughout the decade ending in 2016 within a range of 1 to 4 percentage points.[14] A culture of ethics promotes efficiency, quality, committed employees, loyal customers, and higher profits.

Can you think of a better definition of success?

---

[10] The 2019 Trust Outlook, p. 5. The Trust Edge Leadership Institute, 2018.
[11] CCP Global Human Capital report, 2008, and Gallup, 2012.
[12] H. Boushey and S. Jane Glynn. 2012. "There Are Significant Business Costs to Replacing Employees," *Center for American Progress.*
[13] J. Altman. 2017. "How Much Does Employee Turnover Cost?" *Huffpost.*
[14] P. Georgescu. 2017. "Doing the Right Thing is Just Profitable." *Forbes.*

V. The Current of Prosperity

Culture is like water. It travels from the top down. When leaders invest in creating an ethical culture as the well-spring of good business, the benefits of an ethical mindset flow into our communities and our politics.

This, too, is easier said than done. Many leaders who possess the vision, drive, acumen, and confidence to make savvy business decisions are adept at finding avenues around the law and may even consider themselves above the law. Without a method of checks and balances, the temptation to game the system is almost irresistible.

That's why we have compliance laws. However, when compliance regulations provide a substitute for an ethical mindset, the proposed cure ends up masking the spread of the disease.

And when that happens, compliance becomes the enemy of ethics.

No one said it better than Edmund Burke: *Men of intemperate minds cannot be free. Their passions forge their fetters.* Herein lies the extraordinary wisdom and vision of the United States Constitution. Recognizing the self-serving predisposition of human nature, the Framers created a document not of laws but of legal principles and ideals to foster a culture of ethical consciousness. The same construct applies to business as well. That's why compliance laws only succeed when they rest on a foundation of ethical idealism.

Tragically, both ethics and idealism are hard to find. Over time, a torrent of political acrimony and social anarchy has eroded the bedrock principles of the world's first true democratic republic. An agenda-driven media and the influence of money on elections has created a corrupt political culture unlikely to repair itself.

But the power to shape a healthy *professional* culture still resides in the hands of business and corporate leaders. It is theirs to restore or to abandon.

What is the first step forward? To adopt the language of Hillel's famous aphorism: *The guide for civilized living is ethics. All the rest is commentary; go learn it.*

Learn it from King Solomon; from Socrates; from *Ethics of Fathers*; from Marcus Aurelius; from Thomas Aquinas; from John Locke; from Khalil Gibran; from Phillipa Foot; from Stephen L. Carter; from Rabbi

Lord Jonathan Sacks; from Susan Cain; from Dan Ariely; from Carol Dweck; from Adam Grant; from Brené Brown; from Jonathan Haidt.

Ethical Principle #7: *Like any other discipline, ethics must be studied at the feet of masters.*

We have easy access to a pantheon of moral authorities, ancient and modern, who will show us the way if we're willing to follow their lead. They won't solve our ethical dilemmas for us. But they will do something even better—they will teach us how to grapple with those dilemmas ourselves.

VI. Finding Our Way Forward

The sages warn us: "Don't trust yourself until the day you die."[15] Confidence easily mutates into overconfidence, which leads to arrogance, carelessness, and complacency. Countless stories of true heroes who grew intoxicated with their own success and lost their way fill the pages of history. It's only through continuous self-reflection and reexamination that we can negotiate the ethical questions, large and small, that wait for us around every turn.

Imagine this:

You're turning onto an east–west expressway. The toll collector asks which direction you're traveling. You answer, *west*. He waves you through without charging you. Only when you see the destination sign do you realize that your directional dyslexia has kicked in: You made a mistake; you're actually heading *east*. It was an honest mistake. You want to pay the toll, which is only $2.50. But it will take you close to half an hour to turn around, find your way back to the toll collector, and pay the toll. Your intellect tells you to let it go. It's an insignificant amount. You weren't intentionally being dishonest. Your time is worth more than that. You'll give the same amount to charity when you get home. But your gut tells you that you need to pay. What do you do?

You lost a promotion to a colleague who stole credit for work *you* had done. Now you have the opportunity to implicate him in a scandal he had

---

[15] *Ethics of Fathers* 2:4.

nothing to do with. Logic suggests that he deserves to pay for his previous malfeasance; even if he is innocent of this crime, he is guilty of another. Instinct suggests that committing fraud to punish fraud is no justification. What do you do?

You work for Homeland Security. You have credible evidence of an impending terrorist attack against a major American city. You have in custody the leader of a cell who likely has information that can prevent the attack. Logic suggests that torture is the most effective way to get the information you need and save countless lives. Conscience tells you that if you act like a terrorist you are no better than a terrorist. How do you decide what to do?

Questions like these have no easy answers. But we can't even begin to answer them until we approach them with ethical discipline and integrity. Moreover, the way we deal with the smaller questions will influence the way we deal with the larger ones because, for better or for worse, we are the sum of all our choices. Every decision we make reveals who we are and shapes who we will become.

Once we apply the principles of ethics to our professional lives, we improve the chance that those same principles will seep out into the world of social and political engagement, restoring civil society, providing our communities with a new lease on life, and driving ever greater prosperity.

We don't have to be noble; we just have to be smart. When all is said and done, we'll find that being noble and being smart are truly one and the same.

VII. Taking Action

After identifying the principles of ethics, we have an ethical imperative to apply these principles to our attitudes and our behavior. That application of **ethical actions steps** looks like this:

- **#1: Evaluate informational integrity**. Protect against rational ignorance by seeking out all relevant information both supporting and opposing any position.
- **#2: Evaluate emotional bias**. Protect against groupthink by engaging in civil discourse with those who hold opposing views.

#3: Evaluate logical consistency. Articulate your opinions so those who have not already bought into them can understand them. Rearticulate opposing views to confirm that you understand them and are able to authentically represent them. Through constructive disagreement, determine if the same reasoning supporting one side applies equally to the other.

#4: Cultivate empathy through understanding. Engage ideological adversaries on a personal basis. Learn about their backgrounds, their families, their interests, and their dreams. Learn their stories, independent of their ideologies, and you will become less inclined to divide the world into "us" and "them."

#5: Translate awareness into action. Monitor your own responses, your language and style of speech, your own behavior and ethical discipline. Solicit feedback from objective observers.

#6: Recognize that acting ethically is in your own best interest. Act in the way you would like others to act toward you. Define yourself as a force for good and strive to be a source of positive inspiration.

#7: Learn from a mentor. Seek out models of virtue in articles, books, interviews, or videos—but especially face-to-face. There is no substitute for human interaction with people of quality. As Jim Rohn said, "You are the average of the five people you spend the most time with."

Stop looking for shortcuts, loopholes, and justifications to circumvent the spirit of the law. Seek out the humanity in those with whom you disagree. Demand the same intellectual integrity from yourself that you demand from others. The case studies that follow provide the opportunity to test your own fair-mindedness and moral objectivity. Don't try to justify your preconceptions. Try to discover the truth.

Recognize how bettering yourself betters the world, and how living in a better world makes for a better life. When you do, you set yourself on a course to attain the life of success and happiness you've always dreamed of.

PART 1

Ethical Relationships

Do not despise any person, and do not disdain any thing; for there is no person without his hour and no thing without its place.
—Ethics of Fathers 4:3

The Ugly Truth

You're walking down the hallway of a corporate office building. The elevator door opens in front of you, and out of the elevator steps your next-door neighbor—a nice young lady with whom you're very friendly.

"What are you doing here?" you ask.

She replies, "I'm so excited; I have a great job opportunity. I'm interviewing with a corporate law firm in this office *right here, right now*. How do I look?"

You look her over and think: "*O-M-G. No one should walk into the bathroom looking like that! Did she look in the mirror before she left the house?*"

How do you respond to her question?

Grapple with the Gray

List two or three reasons why you should tell your neighbor she looks great.

List two or three reasons why you should tell your neighbor the truth.

Is there another option?

Having weighed the options, what would you do?

Gray Matters

Consider the effect of telling the truth; what would you accomplish with brutal honesty? If you had caught your neighbor going out her front door, you could have suggested a change of attire while she could actually do something about it. But now it's too late. Telling her the truth will merely make her self-conscious.

On the other hand, telling her she looks great is dishonest. What's more, it denies her the opportunity to learn the importance of self-presentation. When she doesn't get the job, and later contemplates how she might have made a better impression, she's likely to think, "My neighbor told me I looked great; I guess my choice of outfit wasn't the problem."

In awkward situations, many of us naturally turn to deflection: "Oh my gosh, look at the time … gotta run. Good luck!" or "How about those Red Sox?"

The problem with deflection is that it's usually recognized as deflection. It may not be overtly cruel, but most likely it will be interpreted as uncomplimentary and have a deflating effect.

The best option is clever evasion: "You are definitely going to make an impression!" or "Just make sure you show them who you are on the inside!" These responses sound supportive without being untruthful or reinforcing her error. Sometime later, you might offer some advice. Or, she may reflect on her own that you didn't actually compliment her choice of outfit, then reconsider how to dress for future interviews.

The first steps toward an ethical response involve evaluating honesty, benefit, and timing, as well as thinking outside of the binary mindset: "Do I tell the truth or lie?" There is almost always another option.

Be Our Guest

You and your spouse are enjoying a quiet evening at home. You had a challenging week at the office, which culminated in a major success. You decide to celebrate by breaking out an expensive bottle of French wine you received as a gift several years earlier.

As you stand up to fetch the bottle, there's a knock at the door. Another couple you haven't seen in ages were in the neighborhood and, on impulse, decided to drop in.

"We are so glad you came by," you tell your unexpected guests. "In your honor, we're going to open a bottle of wine we've been saving for a special occasion."

Have you done anything wrong?

Grapple with the Gray
  List two or three reasons in favor of claiming that you're honoring your guests.
  List two or three reasons why you should not make this claim.
  Is there another option?
  Having weighed the options, what would you do?

Gray Matters

You might think to yourself, "Why not make my friends feel special? It costs nothing and spreads good feeling throughout the world."

The problem is that deception—any deception—accustoms us to further deception. This is the problem with so-called white lies. It's not always easy to tell when we're lying solely to spare the feelings of others and when we're lying to benefit ourselves. The more little lies we tell, the more easily we will tell bigger and bigger lies as time goes by.

In seeming contradiction, the sages teach that one should always say that the bride is beautiful. But what if she's not?

Philosophically speaking, every bride is beautiful, because marriage is a beautiful institution. Additionally, she is almost certainly beautiful in the eyes of her groom. Finally, no one asked you to editorialize on the aesthetic qualities of the wedding party. You were invited to bring joy to the bride and groom, so find the truth that will contribute to the joyfulness of the occasion and keep your critical observations to yourself.

Most of the time, we don't have to choose between outright honesty and dishonesty. In our case, you should certainly let your guests know how important they are and how pleased you are that they dropped by. But it's just as easy to say, "We were about to open a bottle of wine we've been saving for a special occasion, and we're delighted that you're here to share it with us."

Same result, without the false flattery.

The Gift of Acceptance

A close friend calls you up and explains that his brother and his family are planning a vacation. His brother, however, is struggling financially and can't afford nice accommodations. Your friend wants to help his brother cover the cost of the trip, but he knows his brother is too proud to accept his help.

He has a plan. He'll tell his brother that he has a friend—you—who owns an Airbnb where he can stay for no charge. Your friend will pay you for rental, and his brother will think you're just doing your friend a favor by letting his brother stay there.

You agree.

The brother comes with his family, and they have a wonderful vacation. As they're packing up and preparing to leave, they repeatedly express how grateful they are for your kindness and present you with a thank-you gift—a fancy crystal vase bought at a local curio shop.

Do you accept the gift?[1]

Grapple with the Gray
    List two or three reasons in favor of accepting the gift.
    List two or three reasons why you should refuse the gift.
    Is there another option?
    Having weighed the options, what would you do?

---

[1] Adapted from Y. Zilberstein. 2013. *Veha'arev Na* (Jerusalem, Israel: Philipp Feldheim).

Gray Matters

The problem here is false pretense. It's not your fault, but your friend's brother thinks you've done him a tremendous favor and wants to show his appreciation. Had he known you were being paid, even by someone other than himself, he would have felt no obligation or compulsion to express his gratitude with a pricey gift.

For that reason alone, you should refuse the gift.

However, it's more complicated than that. If you offer no reason for refusing the gift, you might offend him. If you tell him his brother paid for his stay, you might embarrass him and cause strife between brothers.

This might be a good point to discuss the ethics of the entire deception. The precept of charity includes not only helping those unable to help themselves, but doing so in a way that preserves their dignity at the same time. Since your friend cannot help his brother openly, this harmless deception is justifiable to achieve a greater good, all the more so because it in no way benefits your friend himself.

Your involvement in the scheme is even less overt; since you are merely facilitating the deception and are not the instigator, you are one step removed. The problem arises only when you receive actual benefit through the deception by accepting the gift. Unlike our previous case of claiming to open the wine especially for the guest, there is no way to be honest here without risking harm, either by causing embarrassment or strife.

The determining factor here, therefore, becomes what best serves the brother who is the recipient of the charity. True, he will have spent money unnecessarily on the gift, but he did so willingly, believing correctly that he would have spent much more had you not made your residence available to him. Since there is no tactful way to decline the gift, it's best to accept it.

If you know where he bought the vase, theoretically you could ask the owner to cancel the credit card charge and cover it yourself. Of course, that assumes he didn't pay by check or with cash. It also assumes that he won't follow up with the store when he notices that the transaction was canceled. Making up elaborate tales to explain the cancellation is not a good idea, since it adds to and complicates the deception.

Alternatively, you might donate the vase, or its value, to a worthy cause. But if you claim a tax deduction, then you're back to benefiting from the gift itself.

A Bump in the Night

Sylvie and Hannah grew up as best friends. Even after they settled in different cities, they remained in close contact.

After Sylvie became engaged, she was so eager for Hannah to attend her wedding that she offered to pay the airfare for Hannah to participate in the celebration. Hannah left for the airport with plenty of time to spare, but a multi-car accident delayed her arrival. When she finally got to the gate, the plane had not yet taken off, but the agent had already bumped her from the overbooked flight. The agent offered to book Hannah on a flight the next day and gave her a $500 gift card as compensation for her delay.

Since the later flight would not allow Hannah to reach her destination in time to attend Sylvie's wedding, she called off the trip. But who is entitled to the compensation money—Sylvie or Hannah?

Grapple with the Gray
    List two or three reasons why Sylvie should get the money.
    List two or three reasons why Hannah should keep the money.
    Is there another alternative?
    Having weighed the options, how would you resolve the question?

Gray Matters

Why do airlines overbook?

It's a numbers game. They want to be able to allow passengers the privilege to cancel or reschedule up to the last minute. According to one estimate, passengers show up for their reserved seats about 93 percent of the time. That means that if airlines book 107 passengers for every 100 seats, they have a good chance of filling every flight.

Of course, sometimes the odds don't cooperate. That's when people get bumped.

Is it ethical for airlines to overbook? That's a more complicated question.

In one sense, the chance of ending up on an overbooked flight is a price that passengers are willing to pay for the security of being able to rebook or cancel. Then the question becomes: How does the airline determine which passengers get bumped on an overbooked flight?

Common practice has become offering cash incentives to passengers willing to give up their seats to take a later flight. (My wife was delighted when we received $1,400 in prepaid credit cards and a free night at the airport hotel to delay our departure until the next morning; the compensation was well worth our inconvenience.)

That seems to be the critical point here. The airline pays bumped passengers for their inconvenience, calculating that over time it will earn more by filling more seats than it will pay out by paying off passengers to delay their travel plans.

Based on that logic, it seems that Hannah should keep the $500. Indeed, if Hannah would have been able to catch a later flight and still make the wedding, then the money would be indisputably hers, since it was her inconvenience.

However, Hannah was not delayed. Because she missed her flight, she had to cancel her trip altogether. Her inconvenience, as it turns out, was a wasted trip to the airport, which is probably not worth $500. There is also the "inconvenience" to Sylvie, who will miss the participation of her friend in her wedding ceremony.

Needless to say, Sylvie is entitled to recover the cost of Hannah's ticket. If the airline offers a refund or credit, then a reasonable solution is for the two friends to split the $500. If the ticket is lost, then the price should be deducted from the $500 and the friends can split the difference.

Living on the Edge

On June 8, 1985, British climber Simon Yates was descending from the 21,000-foot summit of Siula Grande in the Peruvian Andes when his partner, Joe Simpson, fell and shattered his leg. As blizzard conditions engulfed them, Yates turned to the grueling work of getting his friend down the mountain alive.

For nine hours, Yates labored to lower Simpson by rope down the steep incline 300 feet at a time. Then, Simpson lost purchase and began sliding out of control, his ice axe unable to bite into the powdery snow.

Up above, Yates felt the rope jerk hard and knew that Simpson had gone over the edge. Yates still had control of the rope, literally holding Simpson's life in his hands. But frostbitten and exhausted after the previous day's climb and the present day's ordeal, Yates had no strength to pull his friend up. All he could do was wait helplessly, which he did, as Simpson dangled above the abyss.

But after one hour, Yates felt the snow beneath his feet begin to give way. In moments, he would be pulled down the slope and over the edge, together with Simpson. Instinctively, he reached for his Swiss Army knife and cut the rope, knowing that he was letting his friend fall to his death.

Did Simon Yates do the right thing?

Grapple with the Gray
    List two or three reasons why Yates should have cut the rope.
    List two or three reasons why Yates should not have cut the rope.
    Was there another alternative?
    Having weighed the options, what would you have done?

Gray Matters

In a case like this, it's difficult to separate logic from emotion. That's a good thing. Otherwise, we risk compromising our humanity by reducing moral calculations to mere arithmetic, as we'll examine more closely in a later discussion about self-driving cars.

That being said, we need to retain the ability to separate logic from emotion when circumstances require us to do just that. In this scenario, Simon Yates did everything in his power to save Joe Simpson; allowing himself to be dragged to his death would do nothing to save his friend. It may sound callous, but cutting the rope was the only choice that made sense.

The sages postulate an admittedly contrived scenario to illustrate this point.

Imagine you and a friend are crossing an inhospitable desert beneath a blazing sun. Your friend's canteen sprang a leak, and he lost all his water. You have enough water in your canteen to keep you alive until you make your way to the next oasis, but you don't have enough to share. By giving up half your water, you guarantee that both of you will die. By keeping all the water for yourself, you will survive but will condemn your friend to death.

Many of us could not imagine ourselves refusing to share our water. How would we live with the guilt knowing that we had allowed our friend to perish by keeping our water for ourselves? We might reason that sharing our water is the ultimate act of morality, embracing the noble value of friendship and self-sacrifice while hoping for a miracle to save us both.

But we would be mistaken. Not everything is in our hands to control, not every problem has a solution. Our first responsibility is to ourselves. Only by ensuring our own well-being can we be able to help others. Sacrifice as a matter of duty—for love, for patriotic idealism, for camaraderie, for family—is one thing. But sacrificing our lives for no benefit, regardless of how noble our intentions, is the moral equivalent of self-murder.

We also don't know when our well-intentioned actions might do more harm than good. Ironically, after Simon Yates cut the rope, Joe Simpson landed in a snowbank. He survived the fall and managed to drag himself to safety.

Three years later, Simpson published his memoir, *Touching the Void*. He dedicated the book to Simon Yates, for saving his life.

Who Gets the Bill?

You're pacing back and forth outside your favorite restaurant and talking on your cell phone as you wait for your friend Terry, who's meeting you for lunch. Terry shows up, reaches down to the sidewalk and comes up holding a $50 bill.

"Is this yours?" he asks.

You remember getting change for 100 that morning and, still finishing up your phone conversation, you check your wallet. No 50. "Yeah, that must be mine," you say, thanking Terry as you take the bill and put it in your wallet.

After lunch, you go to your car, reach in your pocket for your keys, and come out with a $50 bill. You recheck your wallet—another $50 bill. You realize that you didn't drop the 50, you merely misplaced it. The one Terry picked up off the ground wasn't yours at all.

Now what do you do? Give the 50 bucks back to Terry or keep it for yourself?[2]

Grapple with the Gray

List two or three reasons in favor of keeping the 50.
List two or three reasons why Terry should get it.
Is there another option?
Having weighed the options, what would you do?

---

[2] Adapted from Y. Zilberstein. 2013. *Veha'arev Na* (Jerusalem, Israel: Philipp Feldheim).

Gray Matters

The law requires you to make every reasonable effort to return lost money or property to its rightful owner. But that refers to a case where the owner can demonstrate ownership, like a wallet with ID, a monogrammed billfold, a distinctive bag, or an easily identifiable object. Since most people don't memorize serial numbers or write personal notes on cash, a single bill can't be traced to any specific owner. Consequently, there is a presumption of immediate ownership by the person who found it.

In this case, because the bill was at your feet it was reasonable for Terry to assume that it might be yours. When you couldn't locate your own fifty, you were justified in assuming that indeed it was yours. There was no dishonest intent, and you did nothing wrong by accepting the bill.

However, had you not misplaced your own $50 bill, Terry would have rightfully kept the bill he found for himself. Therefore, once you recognize the error that brought the fifty into your possession, the ethical thing to do is return it to Terry.

The additional moral challenge here is that Terry will probably have forgotten the incident altogether by the time you discover your mistake—a mistake he will never know about unless he hears it from you. Moreover, the money wasn't Terry's to begin with and, perhaps, you would have looked down in another moment and discovered the bill yourself.

It's easy to rationalize that keeping the fifty is a victimless crime—or no crime at all. Terry hasn't lost anything and doesn't think he has lost anything. And you played a part in the money's discovery; if you'd been standing a few feet away in either direction, someone else would have happened upon the fifty.

The danger of rationalization is that we train ourselves to legitimize fraudulent behavior. By engaging in mental gymnastics to justify self-serving conclusions, we make it easier to blur ethical lines in cases where there's less room for rationalizing, skewing our own moral compass and drifting toward the boundary between ethics and legality.

Returning the fifty to Terry contains its own rewards. He'll be impressed with your honesty. More important, you will have strengthened your ethical muscles, making you better prepared to respond correctly to more precarious ethical dilemmas.

It's a Sure Bet

A king once sent his son on a diplomatic mission to another country. As he finished preparing the young man on matters of negotiation, the king said, "There is one more subject of utmost importance. While you are on this trip, under no circumstances are you to enter into any kind of bet or wager."

Since the prince rarely gambled, his father's warning struck him as odd. Strange though he found the admonition, he readily agreed.

The next day, as he boarded the ship that would carry him abroad, his father bid him safe journey and again cautioned him, "Remember, no matter what, you must not accept a bet."

Perplexed by the king's insistence, but not overly concerned, the prince repeated his assurance.

The prince's mission went smoothly and negotiations with the foreign minister were successfully concluded. As the two of them enjoyed a final meal together, the foreign minister remarked, "You are a very skillful negotiator," he said, "which is all the more impressive because of your handicap."

"What handicap is that?" asked the prince, startled by the remark.

"Why, that you are a hunchback," replied the minister.

The prince looked astonished. "I have no idea what you are talking about," he exclaimed.

"Oh, you conceal it very well," said the minister, "and I apologize for bringing it up, as I'm sure it is a source of embarrassment."

"There is no embarrassment involved," replied the prince, "since I am not a hunchback."

"Between the two of us, there is no need to deny it," insisted the minister. "I am quite adept at noticing details. By the way you walk and the way you carry yourself I can see clearly that you are."

"I'm afraid you are mistaken," replied the prince, beginning to grow angry.

"See here," said the minister, appearing somewhat heated himself. "I pride myself on my ability to notice what others do not. Not only do I say you are a hunchback, but I will bet you a hundred thousand rubles that I am right."

Immediately, the prince remembered his father's warning. But certainly, his father could not have anticipated a circumstance like this one. This was not gambling. This was a sure thing.

Should the prince take the bet?

Grapple with the Gray

    List two or three reasons why the prince should take the bet.
    List two or three reasons why the prince should not take the bet.
    Is there another alternative?
    Having weighed the options, what would you do?

Gray Matters

The story concludes as follows:

The prince accepted the bet and promptly removed his shirt, revealing that he was undeniably not a hunchback.

"Now I am the one who is embarrassed," said the minister as he counted out a large number of bills and handed them over. "I can't understand how I could have been so mistaken. Please accept my apologies with your winnings."

The prince returned home and, upon greeting his father, eagerly recounted the way he had profited a hundred thousand rubles.

Instead of pleasure, the king turned red with anger. "Did I not tell you to refuse any wager?" he demanded. "Let me tell you now that I bet the foreign minister half-a-million rubles that he could not get you to take a bet!"

Ethics is the foundation of trust, just as it is supported by trust. The stability of civil society depends on an implicit social contract, according to which citizens have reason to expect that their neighbors are all committed to the same underlying values of honesty and fair play, that they do not actively seek any opportunity to game the system for their own advantage.

When that trust is eroded, the foundations of society begin to disintegrate as well.

This is even more true with respect to family. On the one hand, we need to know when to take initiative, to evaluate when our instructions may not fully apply to an unexpected circumstance. On the other hand, we have to trust that instructions have been given for a reason, even if—and perhaps, especially if—we don't fully understand the reason behind those instructions, or we think those reasons no longer apply.

In this case, the king's insistence to exact a peculiar promise from his son without explanation was evidence that the king had concerns that he was either unable or unwilling to share with his son. By assuming that he understood the situation better than his father could have anticipated, the prince demonstrated a lack of trust which—in this case at great expense—displayed a lack of ethics.

No Cancellations?

I bumped into my neighbor, a doctor, one morning and asked him about a chronic problem that was flaring up. He suggested I try a couple of over-the-counter products and schedule an appointment with him in his office a month later in case the OTC medicines didn't help.

I saw him again a couple of weeks later and told him that my symptoms had abated. In that case, he said, I didn't need to come in to see him.

He then asked me not to cancel my appointment. He assured me that I wouldn't be charged for missing the visit. However, his group required him to see a minimum number of patients each week, and if I kept my appointment scheduled that would lighten his workload.

His request put me in a quandary. Was it ethical of him to ask me not to cancel an appointment I no longer needed? If not, would it be ethical for me to become his conspirator in doing just that?

Grapple with the Gray

List two or three reasons for canceling the appointment.
List two or three reasons for not canceling the appointment.
Was there another option?
Having weighed the options, what would you have done?

Gray Matters

I did not cancel the appointment. And I'm still not sure whether or not I did the right thing.

The doctor had done me a favor by dispensing free medical advice. It seemed unappreciative not to honor his request, as it did not require me to commit an overtly unethical act.

There's also a certain amount of unknown information. Many practices require their doctors to see an unreasonable number of patients, sometimes compromising quality of care to meet a bottom line. Maybe lightening the doctor's load would actually increase the quality of care he would be able to give his other patients.

If all this sounds like rationalizing, it is.

One of the obstacles we face by aspiring to be ethical is the challenge of living in a society where ethics is not a widely held value—or, at least, where others are less sensitive than we are to ethical compromise. We have to live with our neighbors, our friends, and our family, which forces us to evaluate the time, place, and manner of how we respond when their actions may drift into the ethical twilight regions.

The sages enumerate 48 ways of wisdom, one of which is to "love rebuke." Ethical people appreciate the opportunity to be made more aware of their missteps in order to correct them and become even more ethically sensitive. But experience and knowledge of human nature inform us that rebuke is rarely received with appreciation. Unless it is offered in precisely the right time, place, tone, and measure, we can appear superior or sanctimonious in a way that ends up damaging our relationships.

It's also easy to rationalize that crimes of omission are not as serious as crimes of commission. In general, that may be true. But they are still crimes.

Certainly, the most effective way to give rebuke is to be a model of ethical behavior. But sometimes that becomes more complicated when our own standards of morality have an impact on others who lack our moral sensitivity.

In the words of Professor Albus Dumbledore: "It takes a great deal of bravery to stand up to our enemies, but just as much to stand up to our friends."

In fact, the best definition of a friend is someone willing to tell us when we are wrong. Had the doctor been a friend rather than just an acquaintance, I might have questioned the morality of not canceling my appointment. Perhaps I should have raised the subject anyway and given the doctor an opportunity to defend his request. Indeed, perhaps he had an ethical explanation that hadn't occurred to me and would have broadened my own ethical perspective.

Setting standards for ourselves does not give us free license to demand or even expect those standards from others. It's a complicated balancing act to accept ethical ambivalence from those around us without becoming ambivalent ourselves.

I still question whether I did the right thing. That it still bothers me might be the clearest indication that I did not.

Bliss is Ignorance

Imagine being in a relationship where you and your significant other never hurt each other's feelings, never get into arguments, accept each other's flaws unconditionally, spend every free moment together, and never look at another member of the opposite sex.

Does this sound like your dream of a perfect life? What would you pay or do to make it a reality?

Do you know any couples living a life of blissful commitment like the one just described? Do you wonder why this kind of relationship seems rare, if not unknown? Have you ever known a couple you thought was blissfully happy, only to learn that they had broken up and gone their separate ways?

Would it surprise you to learn that these apparently ideal behaviors might actually be symptoms of a toxic relationship?

Grapple with the Gray

List two or three reasons why you might like this kind of relationship.

List two or three reasons why this kind of relationship might not be healthy.

Is there a different way you would describe a perfect relationship?

After thoughtful consideration, what could you do or have done to improve a present or past relationship?

Gray Matters

It's a law of physics that without friction, nothing moves. A healthy relationship is one with give and take, push and pull, conflict and resolution. That's all part of what it means to be a human being.

How do you avoid hurting another person's feelings? One way is to never say anything of any consequence. The other way is to remain emotionally at arm's length, never getting close enough to cause pain.

As we have already described, relationships are built on trust. Love, whether romantic or platonic, means that I care enough about you to let you know when you're wrong. By doing so, I give you the opportunity to address a problem and thereby protect you from coming to harm or inflicting harm on others. Sure, it stings, like a doctor's hypodermic needle. But just as a doctor gets better at giving injections with practice, so too do we get better at gentle chastisement over time, making mistakes, learning from them, taking responsibility for our errors, and expressing remorse when we cause hurt.

The only doctor who never causes pain is the one who never practices medicine. With rare exception, the only companion who never causes hurt is the one who never gets close enough to express authentic love.

It's the same with arguments. Different people have different points of view, different priorities, different likes and dislikes. Perpetual agreement usually masks deep insecurity and sets the stage for a breakdown or an explosion later, if not sooner. The ability to work through disagreements without inflicting needless pain is part of how we mature in our relationships and learn to balance our respective needs.

Part of that means acknowledging flaws—in ourselves and in the ones we love. We're all human, and therefore imperfect. But acceptance of imperfection is not an excuse for complacency. We need to aspire to do better, just as we need to encourage and help those we care about to strive toward becoming better as well.

A relationship is formed by the connection of two individuals. But that does not require us to sacrifice our individuality. Just the opposite: The more secure I become in who I am, the better equipped I am to contribute to the partnership we have with each other. In any partnership, time apart is essential to preserving the sense of individual self that keeps partnerships healthy.

Human attraction is a law of the universe, which means that sometimes we may find ourselves attracted to others who are not available to us. President Jimmy Carter was widely ridiculed for commenting that he had lusted after other women in his heart. However, the interviewer who asked the question had been fishing for some admission of infidelity, presumably to puncture Mr. Carter's persona as a man of faith and virtue.

Coming up empty, the interviewer finally resorted to asking whether the president had ever *thought* about another woman. Aside from Mr. Carter's clumsy phrasing, his answer was spot-on: We can't control how we feel, but we can control how we act. Resisting temptation is the hallmark of faithfulness, strengthening both character and commitment.

We are not meant to be perfect; we are meant to strive toward perfection. The messiness of intimacy refines our souls so that they can become more deeply bound to one another.

PART 2

Ethical Business

Commitment to duty shall save the upright; but the faithless shall be trapped by their own schemes.

—Proverbs 11:6

It's All in Your Mind

Rabbi Safra was one of the leading sages in Babylon about 1700 years ago. He was also a diamond merchant who, on one occasion, acquired a particularly large and valuable stone.

Hearing of Rabbi Safra's acquisition, another gem merchant approached him one day after prayer services and offered to buy the stone at what he considered a fair price. The merchant did not realize that Rabbi Safra had not yet finished reciting his own silent prayers, which he refused to interrupt even at the risk of losing the deal.

Receiving no answer, the merchant concluded that he had offended the rabbi by not offering enough for the stone, and so he increased his price. When the rabbi still did not reply, the merchant raised his offer even higher.

Finally, Rabbi Safra concluded his prayers. "I will sell you the stone," he told the merchant. "But I will sell it to you at the first price you offered."

"I don't understand," the merchant replied.

"When you made your first offer, I thought to myself that it was a fair price. The reason I didn't answer was because I could not interrupt my prayers. But once I made up my mind that I would accept your first offer, it would be wrong of me to accept anything more than that."

Should the rabbi have revealed this information, or should he have said nothing and sold his stone for the best price he could get?

Grapple with the Gray
    List two or three reasons in favor of accepting the final offer.
    List two or three reasons in favor of accepting the original offer.
    Is there another option?
    Having weighed the options, what would you do?

Gray Matters

Among my favorite movies is the original version of *The Magnificent Seven*, with Yul Brynner and Steve McQueen. In one pivotal scene, some of the villagers have a change of heart and ask the gunslingers they hired to protect their town to leave. Several of the gunmen suggest they should do just that.

Chris: You forget one thing. We took a contract.
Vin: It's sure not the kind any court would enforce.
Chris: That's just the kind you've got to keep.

What's always fascinated me about this dialogue is how hired guns are debating the ethics of defending a town full of people who no longer want to be defended, of honoring a contract they accepted for payment far below their normal fee that the other side wants to annul.

The subtext of the story is this: In order to live with the ruthlessness of their chosen profession, the gunmen compensate by setting higher standards for themselves in other aspects of their lives. Implicitly, they understand that if they are going to operate outside the law, they have to create their own legal code to prevent them from descending into moral anarchy and forfeiting their own humanity.

True, it's just a movie. But the sentiment expressed by the characters is one immediately relevant to real life. If we abdicate moral authority to a system of laws, then we conflate two entirely different principles: on one side, the utilitarian purpose of our legal system as a baseline for preserving social order; on the other, the essence of morality—to elevate mankind toward the realization of its innate noble character.

As a rule, it's useful to define ethics as the awareness of how our actions influence the world around us. The case of Rabbi Safra however, teaches the need to remain aware of the impact our actions have on ourselves.

Every time we act with even the smallest measure of deception or lack of integrity, we damage the sensitivity of our own moral compass by diminishing our own commitment to honesty and truth. If you've already made up your mind to complete a deal at a fair price, you're not being true to yourself by taking advantage of circumstances to exact something extra from the transaction, even if you are entirely within your legal rights to do so.

Keeping our word—even when it's unspoken—is foundational to the well-being of a civil society. It is in line with the classic definition of integrity: doing the right thing, even when no one else is watching.

On the Wing

On September 7, 2019, a United Airlines passenger asked to move from his crowded row to an unoccupied row further up. He was not requesting a first-class seat, but merely to take an identical economy seat a few rows forward.

He was told *no*. Those seats, he was informed, were for Economy Plus customers who paid a premium so they could board early and have access to seats closer to the cabin door. To let a regular economy passenger take one of those seats would not be fair to the customers who had paid for them.

The customer messaged the airline, arguing that the seats were empty, and all the passengers had boarded. No one would lose anything by allowing him to move; indeed, other passengers—both him and his crowded neighbors—could have a more pleasant flight.

The airline responded with this message:

"The customers who choose to pay for Economy Plus are then afforded that extra space. If you were to purchase a Toyota, you would not be able to drive off with a Lexus, because it was empty."

Who is right—the passenger or the airline?

Grapple with the Gray

List two or three reasons why the airline should have allowed the move.

List two or three reasons why the airline should not have allowed the move.

Did the airline have another option?

Having weighed the options, what would you have done?

Gray Matters

In all likelihood, the same passenger would never have asked permission to move from economy class to an empty seat in first class. Why not? Because that would clearly be unfair not only to the passengers who paid for more comfortable seats and more amenities in first class but also to other economy passengers who have just as much right to an upgrade. Indeed, the airline could replace larger first-class seats with a larger number of smaller economy seats, but chooses to provide an option for flyers who can afford more luxury.

But what are Economy Plus passengers really paying for? Their seats and the service they receive are exactly the same as in regular economy class. Instead, they pay a small premium for the convenience of earlier boarding and the security of knowing they will not have to struggle to find a seat to their liking, as well as being able to deplane more quickly.

Once the doors close, however, allowing customers in crowded seats to enjoy a more comfortable flight has no effect on either the premium customers, who got what they paid for, or on the airline, which incurs no further cost regardless of where passengers sit. What's more, when a passenger in a crowded row moves forward, the passengers who shared his row also benefit from having more room themselves.

The airline's comparison to a Toyota and a Lexus is mere deflection and, frankly, insulting. All cars on a lot are empty until sold; unlike a car, the same seat is sold again and again on each flight. Using clearly flawed logic for rhetorical effect shows contempt for both the other party and for the ideal of conflict resolution.

The underlying principle here is this: Where it costs one party nothing to benefit another, that should be seen as a win–win. There is also the once-universal principle that the customer is always right, as well as the sociological truism that good behavior by one party promotes better behavior from others.

In this case, the opposite occurred. In the end, the flight attendant did allow the passenger to move up. But this was not customer service; it merely made the flight attendant's job easier by appeasing a cantankerous passenger. It also reinforced among the other passengers the perception that the way to get what you want is to make a fuss, which is a mindset that makes everyone's world less pleasant.

How much better it would be if we recognize opportunities to benefit others at no or little cost to ourselves. By doing so, we encourage others to demonstrate the same kind of thoughtfulness, thereby making everyone's world a bit warmer.

Lights Out

In July 1977, a lightning strike in Westchester County set off a power outage that plunged New York City into 25 hours of darkness. Flights were canceled, baseball games suspended, and subway trains ground to a halt. Looting spread through neighborhoods in Brooklyn and the Bronx, along with hundreds of fires set by arsonists.

Imagine that you were walking from your office in Brooklyn to catch the subway home when the lights went out. Within moments, you hear the sound of shattering glass and see flames rising up into the sky. A taxi pulls up beside you, and the cabbie yells, "You want to get out of here?"

It's a $30 ride home, but you consider it a bargain. As you climb in, the driver says, "For a hundred bucks I'll take you wherever you want to go." The crowds seem to be growing more unruly by the moment. "All right," you say, "whatever you want."

When the cabbie pulls up in front of your house, you say, "Listen. I'll pay the regular fare, and I'll even give you a tip. But I'm not paying you a hundred dollars. That's extortion."

"A deal's a deal," the cabbie replies. "You agreed to the price. You have to pay."

Who's right?

Grapple with the Gray

    List two or three reasons why you have to pay what you agreed.
    List two or three reasons why you only have to pay the regular fare.
    Was there another alternative?
    Having weighed the options, what would you do?

Gray Matters

First, we need to address the ethics of price gouging. In the case of popular sporting events or Broadway shows, it's not unusual to hear stories of tickets selling for many times face value. One might argue that this is simply supply and demand. If people are willing to pay inflated prices, why should there be any objection to holding out for whatever the market will bear?

There are two ethical objections to this reasoning. In theory, overcharging can accelerate inflation. Rising prices in one commodity might draw prices of other goods and services up with them, adversely affecting working people on a limited budget.

Sociologically, a healthy culture is one whose members exchange goods and services for a fair price, with all parties benefiting from a mutually acceptable standard of value. When merchants become cutthroat in an effort to wring every last penny out of every transaction, the trust necessary to sustain a viable economy is lost, and society grows increasingly unstable.

In short, there's nothing wrong with getting a good deal, but not when doing so takes advantage of others or causes the fabric of society to fray. In certain times and places, the law itself has prohibited the practice of "scalping." And virtually everyone shared the outrage directed at the baristas who charged $130 for three cases of bottled water to emergency responders on 9/11.

Nevertheless, there is still the matter of keeping one's word. Many of us grew up hearing our parents lament the "good old days" when a man was as good as his word and a handshake was the only contract necessary. Even if overcharging is unethical, once I agree to pay an inflated fee, am I not obliged to follow through on the bargain?

Under normal circumstances, that would seem to be so, even if I'm doing business with someone who is less than upright.

But our case is not normal. Many states have what are known as Good Samaritan laws, requiring citizens to intervene where they can by coming to the aid of others in need. Such laws are built upon the scriptural mandate, "You shall not stand idle over your brother's blood."[1] When my neighbor is in need, I need to help if I can.

---

[1] Leviticus 19:16.

Consequently, the cab driver has an ethical responsibility to help a pedestrian in danger. He is certainly allowed to charge his regular fare. But he has no right to capitalize on the desperation of others and exploit their desperation for his own profit.

Moreover, because you have as much responsibility to save your own life as the life of another, you would be permitted to agree to his price up front, even with no intention—or obligation—to actually pay it.

Happy Brith-day

You order a cake for your daughter's birthday party. You pick up the cake on the afternoon of the big day and hide it until the party, then bring it out to the table once the festivities have begun. Only then do you discover that your daughter's name, Harper, has been miswritten in icing as Harpie.

As upsetting as this may be, you need the cake for the party, so you go ahead and serve it. The next day you return to the cake store to complain.

Are you entitled to your money back?

Grapple with the Gray
  List two or three reasons why you deserve your money back.
  List two or three reasons why you don't deserve your money back.
  Is there another alternative?
  Having weighed the options, what would you do if you were the shopkeeper?

Gray Matters

If you would have noticed the error in time to return to the store, there is no question that the storekeeper would be obligated to fix the error, provide a new cake, or refund your money.

However, you had the party and ate the cake, so you did benefit from the flour, water, sugar, and artistry that went into the cake's production. It was an honest mistake, and the actual damage to you and your daughter was minimal. (If she and her friends were old enough to know what a harpy is, perhaps a bit more.)

You also share some degree of negligence yourself for not examining the cake before you left the shop. You may have a legal claim against the shopkeeper to refund the cost of the custom lettering, but ethically you should not expect a full refund.

That being said, customer service and customer relations are part of good business. It is therefore both ethical and a best practice to offer the customer some accommodation, most likely a partial refund or store credit for some future purchase.

In cases such as these (some of which we will soon examine), there is an inclination to exaggerate the damage and, even worse, presume the worst possible intent, often with the objective of filing legal actions that often end in disproportionately large decisions or settlements. In such scenarios, the law is used as a weapon to extort money from well-intentioned people. The result is more lawsuits, less goodwill, and less civility.

The ability and willingness to evaluate partial guilt and proportionate damage is critical to arriving at an ethical compromise.

Checking Out

True story:

After 11 years working as office manager for a medium-sized company, Charlene found a position with another company offering a higher salary and improved benefits. Her future employer wanted her to start in 2 weeks, but her current contract required her to give 4 weeks' notice.

She went to her employer, explained the situation, and asked to be released from the 4-week notice restriction. Her employer flatly refused. When she explained that the job might not be available to her if she did not start in 2 weeks, her employer said that if she left her position early she would be placed on a no-rehire list, she would not be paid for her remaining paid-time-off, and that she would receive no end-of-the-year bonus. (It was mid-December).

The next Friday was payday. Charlene waited until her paycheck cleared, then stopped coming to work. She never called in or let anyone know about her absence, leaving her former colleagues scrambling to cover her responsibilities. No one in the office ever heard from her after that.

Grapple with the Gray
    List two or three reasons to support Charlene's actions.
    List two or three reasons to support the employer's position.
    Is there a way to resolve the stand-off?
    Having weighed both sides, who's right and who's wrong?

Gray Matters

There's so much wrong in this story that it's painful to recount.

If Charlene had worked loyally and faithfully for 11 years, it's irrelevant that her contract requires her to give a month's notice. Basic gratitude and social conscience demand that an employer not attempt to hold an employee hostage to the point where she stands to lose a better job option. If, after a decade of work, there has not been sufficient opportunity for advancement, the employer should graciously and gracefully wish the employee well.

Of course, it's possible that short notice will leave the employer short-handed. But the civil thing to do is seek some kind of compromise. Perhaps Charlene could come in twice a week, for a few hours each day, or telecommute part-time. Presenting an all-or-nothing ultimatum might be contractually defensible, but it lacks sensitivity, integrity, and appreciation.

It's understandable that Charlene would want to collect her final paycheck before checking out. But she didn't even finish the 2 weeks she asked for, which is the norm in most industries for giving notice. She might have even gone the extra mile and offered to come in for her last few days without being paid, to make up for her early withdrawal.

At the very least, she should have called to say she wasn't coming in, rather than leaving her coworkers high and dry, wondering if she would return and having to pick up her slack. No matter how miffed she might (justifiably) have been at her employer, she had no right to make her colleagues suffer by adding to her boss's lack of civility with her own.

One of the many problems with unethical behavior is that it tends to promote more unethical behavior. Why, we ask ourselves, should we go the extra mile when others won't even go an extra yard? In the end, we all end up losers, and we infect those around us with the bitterness we unnecessarily spread.

A Drop in the Cup

If your memory stretches back to February 1992, you may recall the case of Stella Liebeck. The 79-year-old resident of Albuquerque, New Mexico, spilled her coffee in her lap while holding it between her legs in the car, then turned around and sued the McDonald's restaurant that served her for $4 million.

The public was outraged, all the more so when the jury awarded Ms. Liebeck $2.86 million in damages. I remember thinking to myself—here we go again; irresponsible individuals blaming others for their own mistakes, frivolous lawsuits, and runaway juries. When will the madness end?

Eventually, the full story began to emerge. McDonald's served its coffee at over 180 degrees Fahrenheit, some 30 degrees hotter than most restaurants. In the previous decade, McDonald's had received countless complaints that its coffee was too hot. Some 700 lawsuits targeted the corporation, many of which were settled for a combined half-million dollars.

Ms. Liebeck suffered burns over 16 percent of her body, nearly half of them third degree burns. She underwent skin grafts and required a stay of 8 days in the hospital, and another 3 weeks under her daughter's care before she was able to function on her own.

Initially, she did not file suit against McDonald's, but merely asked the company to reimburse her $18,000 for medical expenses and her daughter's lost wages. The company responded by offering her $800.

The jury assessed Ms. Liebeck's medical expenses, pain, and suffering at $200,000. Then, finding McDonald's 80 percent responsible, it awarded damages of $160,000, plus another $2.7 million in punitive damages—roughly equal to the restaurant's coffee revenue over 2 days.

Grapple with the Gray

    List two or three reasons why the jury decision is fair.
    List two or three reasons why the jury decision is unfair.
    Was there another alternative?
    Having weighed the options, how would you have voted as a juror on the case?

Gray Matters

McDonald's argued that it serves its coffee at a high temperature so it will stay hot longer for commuters on their way to work. This may at first appear to be a reasonable accommodation in the interest of customer service. However, drinking hot coffee while driving is itself an act of questionable wisdom. And while the restaurant is not responsible for the poor choices of its customers, increasing the risk of serious injury for a benefit of minimal value is not a strategy found in the pages of any ethical playbook.

We all do foolish things, betting the small odds of catastrophe against the expectation of immediate convenience. Ms. Liebeck lost that bet when she spilled coffee in her lap. McDonald's lost that bet by selling superheated coffee. The jury acknowledged the complicity of both parties, but held McDonald's to a higher level of responsibility for creating conditions in which a minor accident produced a critical injury.

To a larger degree, the jury held McDonald's culpable for its response. Many corporations recognize that occasional accidents for which they are not completely responsible may result in disproportionate damage to their clients and customers. While refusing to acknowledge responsibility, they often agree to cover medical expenses and recovery, both as a gesture of goodwill and also as a matter of good business.

McDonald's offer of $800 was not merely unjust; it was insulting, and the company knew it. Perhaps the decision-makers at McDonald's assumed that a 79-year-old woman was not going to cause them much trouble and could be bought off cheaply. The jurors apparently concluded that civic responsibility translated into actual liability. Their legal verdict was built on a solid ethical foundation.

The initial public reaction to the story prompts a further discussion about the twin matters of judicial excess and judicial reporting.

In 1995, when Ira Gore, Jr., brought his new BMW into a shop for custom detailing, the detailer detected that the car's paint job was not entirely original. It eventually came out that this car and a thousand others had been damaged by acid rain while being shipped from Germany, and that BMW had repaired the damaged paint without disclosing this information to the customers. In response, an Alabama jury awarded Mr. Gore $4,000 in compensatory damages and $4 million in punitive damages.

Let's accept that the actual reduction in the value of the car was $4,000. And let's assume that BMW was less than honest by not disclosing the repair job.

But in what reality can this modest transgression be evaluated at $4 million? Indeed, Mr. Gore would never have known about the repainting if not for the trained eye of the detailer, and he never would have incurred any financial loss unless he later sold it to a third party with similar expertise.

It's arguable that BMW should be punished on a large scale to discourage similar deception in the future. But why should a single consumer be the sole beneficiary of that punishment?

The case received national attention, drawing the ire of Americans all across the country, as well it should have. The collective sense of outrage led to the passage of legislation capping punitive damage awards, which is not always a good thing. In some cases, the actual monetary damage might be modest while the intangible harm is enormous and the corruption egregious.

This is why ethical values and ethical deliberation are so essential to a healthy civil society. Every case is distinct from every other, which means that every decision must be evaluated on its own merits, under the guidance of judicial wisdom and judicial restraint. Both outlandish and insubstantial verdicts erode public respect for the system, thereby undermining respect for the law in general.

This is where journalistic responsibility comes in. Cases of excess, like the BMW decision, should be broadcast to highlight judicial irresponsibility. But cases like that of Stella Liebeck, so easily satirized, must be carefully reported with complete detail and context.

Justice is elusive and, in this world, unattainable. By calibrating our collective moral compass, we won't get everything right; but we will get closer to consistently equitable outcomes.

State of Mind

I brought a pair of slacks into a new alteration shop to have them hemmed. I returned a week later to pick them up. When I handed the proprietor my check, she saw that my bank was located out of town and refused to accept the check.

I told her—truthfully—that my bank is one of the most respected financial institutions in the country, but she wasn't interested. It was her policy, she said, never to accept out-of-town checks. I replied that my local address was printed on the check, but that wasn't good enough for her.

I then asserted that if she had such a fussy policy about accepting checks, it was her obligation to post a policy sign to that effect or otherwise inform me of such when I dropped off the slacks; since she had not made that stipulation known, it was only proper that she accept the check rather than inconveniencing me to leave and make a second trip to pay in cash.

She refused. Who was right?

Grapple with the Gray
- List two or three reasons that justify the store owner's refusal to accept the check.
- List two or three reasons why she should have accepted it.
- Was there another alternative?
- Having weighed the options, what would you do if you were the proprietor?

Gray Matters

It's quite possible that the proprietor had gotten burned in the past, having accepted an out-of-town check that bounced with no recourse for recovering her loss. It's entirely reasonable, although not particularly common, to demand local checks to ensure a measure of security.

The location of the bank is something different. A respected federal bank that operates nationally without local branches might be more secure than a small, local institution. Refusal to accept a check because the bank is located out of state is not something any patron might reasonably anticipate.

Service providers are within their rights to impose any conditions they deem necessary to protect the security of their businesses. What they don't have is the right to place an undue burden on customers without warning the customers in advance.

This requires notifying customers up front of any policy that might affect or inconvenience them, especially if that policy deviates from normal business practice. Having failed to alert me up front that my check might not be accepted, the proprietor should have conceded that she had not given me fair warning and accepted the check with an explanation that, in the future, she would only accept checks from local banks.

By refusing to do so, she may have protected herself from the slim chance that my check would bounce. But she also lost my business forever.

In his classic work *Path of the Just*, the 17th-century ethicist Rabbi Moshe Chaim Luzzato offers the pithy observation that "there is fear and there is fear." In other words, there are reasonable dangers we need to account for as we proceed through the normal, day-to-day business of our lives. To disregard such commonsense precautions as looking before crossing the street and not opening our doors at night to strangers is to put our safety needlessly at risk.

However, to indulge wild fantasies about everything that could possibly go wrong and attempt to guard against every contingency is equally foolish, and a sure recipe for making ourselves dysfunctionally neurotic and unbearable company for those closest to us.

An ethical mindset influences every aspect of our lives, guiding us to balance all our decisions as we walk the precarious path between looking out for ourselves and remaining sensitive to others.

Many Happy Returns?

Let's face it: We're all a little neurotic. But when quirks and mild aversions grow into crippling phobias, psychologists may search for novel and creative solutions.

As an antidote for pathological shyness, one psychologist instructed patients to go into department stores and engage salespeople by asking for product information and advice. In some cases, patients were instructed to make purchases, then come back a few days later to return the merchandise.

The concept is simple. Through repeated interactions of this kind, patients gradually become comfortable with approaching strangers, asking for information, and asserting themselves in the normal give and take of daily human discourse.

However, this form of therapy depends on the unknowing collaboration of store personnel, potentially interfering with their job of attending to paying customers, distracting them from other work, creating extra work in dealing with returns and restocking, and possibly costing them commissions from real customers.

Is it ethical for the psychologist to treat the patient in a way that might cause even a minor loss and inconvenience to the store and its sales force?[2]

Grapple with the Gray
    List two or three reasons in defense of this kind of treatment.
    List two or three reasons why the psychologist should not prescribe these treatments.
    Did the psychologist have another option?
    Having weighed the options, what would you do?

---

[2] Adapted from Y. Zilberstein. 2013. *Veha'arev Na* (Jerusalem, Israel: Philipp Feldheim).

Gray Matters

According to Jewish law, it is forbidden to go into a store to ask the price of an item after having purchased it elsewhere merely to ascertain whether or not you got a good deal. To do so not only distracts store personnel from what might be more profitable activities but also raises the false hope of actually making a sale.

However, the world of sales and marketing is perpetually evolving. There was a time when all sales were final. Now that returns are common, finding a lower price after making a purchase could indeed lead to returning the original item and buying it elsewhere for the lower price.

What's more, sales are no longer just about single interactions and purchases. They are about relationships and brand loyalty. A pleasant interaction today could lead to many sales in months and years to come.

Retailers also know that even when customers fully intend to return a purchase, they often fail to follow up. They may decide to keep the merchandise, or they may never get around to bringing it back.

Finally, most people are happy to help others when it requires little investment in time or energy. If the store owner and personnel knew that they were helping a patient develop a healthier mental outlook through a few minutes of interaction, they would probably be more than willing to cooperate.

To that end, it might be ethical as well for the psychologist to alert the owners or managers of a few nearby stores that he would be sending his patients their way and ask for their permission and cooperation.

Say Cheese

Having entered our age of self-absorption, all manner of social phenomena have appeared that would have been incomprehensible only a few years ago. It is now common for prospective customers to enter high-end clothing stores and try on designer apparel, not with the intent to buy but in order to take selfies they can later post to their social media pages.

Is this case different from the previous case, since it is motivated solely for ego gratification rather than mental health? Or is it the same, since retailers know that trying on clothes leads to sales and customer experience leads to customer loyalty?

Grapple with the Gray

List two or three reasons why it is acceptable to try on the clothes.
List two or three reasons why it is unacceptable to try on the clothes.
Is there another alternative?
Having weighed the options, what would you do?

Gray Matters

Are these last two scenarios the same, or are they different?

Yes, and yes.

From the point of view of the retailer, the more time a shopper spends in the store, the better, even if that shopper came in with no intention to buy. Moreover, when other shoppers see a customer trying on inventory, they are more likely to try something on themselves.

So from the point of view of the retailer, there's no problem at all trying on the latest fashions to make yourself look better on your Facebook page.

That being said, when we treat other people as tools for our own gratification, we incrementally chip away at the foundations of our own humanity. By using another person's place of business as a means of indulging my own ego, we increase our predisposition for treating people like things in other situations.

You might begin by asking yourself what kind of people you want to impress by showing yourself off in name-brand clothes. And if you absolutely must take the selfie, at least you should ask permission from the shopkeeper—who will almost certainly permit it. With the minimal effort of asking permission, you eliminate the attitude of deception and entitlement that are so corrosive to the content of your character.

When my daughter was in high school, she and a friend were perusing the racks in a local clothing store when a saleswoman offered them a gift if they would try on a new brand of jeans. They declined, explaining that, as Orthodox Jews, they wear only skirts and dresses. The salesperson persisted, saying that they could help her out, since she received a bonus for every customer who tried on a pair of jeans.

Clearly, the promoters did not care why customers tried on the jeans; in their minds, it was all a numbers game. Since my daughter and her friend were entirely up-front, there was nothing unethical about them trying on the jeans and accepting the gift.

Two-Faced

It was a fine day in August somewhere in the Caribbean when Michelle Anne Crack decided to visit the cruise liner spa for a massage. According to Ms. Crack, the therapist in the spa offered her a facial treatment at a special price. Ms. Crack initially declined, but after a persistent sales pitch from the therapist, she agreed to the facial.

According to her report, she then signed a ticket for $29 50.

When she received the paperwork, she discovered that the price listed was $2,950.00. Ms. Crack insists that the amount was altered after she signed the agreement.

When she complained to the ship's duty manager, he offered her a partial refund of $590. Subsequently, she wrote to the cruise company, which refunded the full price of the treatment and offered the following apology:

> We're so sorry to learn of the confusion surrounding the pricing for your Medi-Spa Service. Our company policy is to confirm the price verbally (sic) and twice in writing (on the consent form and receipt) prior to administering the service. We're sorry to learn that this may not have happened.

We need not debate whether outright fraud is ethical, or even legal. But let's give as much benefit of the doubt as we can.

Perhaps the therapist had no intention to deceive when quoting the price of "twenty-nine-fifty." Perhaps Ms. Crack, assuming the treatment was worth about thirty dollars, misread the paperwork.

But even if the "confusion" really was just a case of misunderstanding, are there still ethical considerations at play?

Grapple with the Gray

- List two or three reasons in defense of the therapist's and the cruise line's conduct.
- List two or three reasons why Ms. Crack had good reason to complain.
- Might the cruise line have handled the situation differently?
- Having weighed the options, if you were Ms. Crack, what would you have done?

Gray Matters

If you walk into a car dealership and see a new Maserati priced at $3,000, you know something is wrong. If you see a Ford Escort priced at $300,000, you know something is wrong. There are certain expectations based on common knowledge which, if unmet, set alarms ringing in the mind of any typical buyer. It then becomes the ethical responsibility of the seller to explain the inconsistency.

A specially priced facial treatment on a $3,000 cruise has no business costing $3,000. If it does, it had better be something extraordinary, and whatever makes it special had better be presented in large font and bold type, as should the price tag.

In this case, there should have been no room for misunderstanding. Indeed, the hard-sell tactics Ms. Clark claimed she was subjected to are of dubious morality under any circumstance. But as a passenger on a name-brand luxury cruise line, Ms. Clark had no reason to suspect that she would be manipulated into signing away a month's pay when she walked into the spa and asked for a massage.

Almost as bad was the cruise line's classic non-apology apology for regretting the "confusion surrounding the pricing." When a customer feels—all the more so for good reason—that a vendor has acted in bad faith, that's the time for the vendor to not only offer a hasty and sincere apology but go the extra mile by appeasing the customer and demonstrating that the same bad faith will never be visited on any other customers in the future.

Invisible Customers

Benny was widely recognized as a whiz kid by his fellow economics students, asking all the right questions in class and coming up with smart answers that impressed even the professor.

Over the summer, he arranged his notes into a short primer on economic theory, which he self-published in hope of making a few bucks by selling them to incoming freshmen at the start of the fall semester. He left a couple of dozen copies with the owner of a popular off-campus bookstore.

A week later, the store owner called to tell Benny the books had sold out and he needed more copies.

"Wow," said Benny, "I had no idea they would sell that fast."

The shopkeeper grinned. "I have a secret system," he said. "I post a preorder sign-up sheet in the school library. I write about 15 fake names on the sheet, which makes the book look like a hot item and gets more people to order it so they won't miss out on something good."[3]

Grapple with the Gray

    List two or three reasons why the shopkeeper was wrong to do what he did.

    List two or three reasons why the shopkeeper did nothing wrong.

    If the shopkeeper was wrong, does Benny in any way share the blame or guilt?

    Having weighed the options, what should Benny do now?

---

[3] Adapted from Y. Zilberstein. 2013. *Veha'arev Na* (Jerusalem, Israel: Philipp Feldheim).

Gray Matters

In the publishing industry, a creative marketing tactic is sometimes employed to establish "social proof." Authors—or their surrogates—buy large numbers of their own books at around 3:00 am. Then, when their Amazon ratings momentarily spike in the book's narrowly defined niche, they take screenshots and proudly proclaim, **#1 Amazon bestseller**.

Widely condemned as unethical, the practice does not involve any technical fraud or outright criminality. Authors are allowed to buy copies of their own book like anyone else, and the Amazon ratings system doesn't know or care who purchases the book.

The problem is the manipulation of the system to create the false perception of popularity, thereby deceiving potential customers into believing that, since many others have invested in the book, it must be worth buying and reading.

We expect publishers to use hyperbolic adjectives in their marketing copy and sales promotions. We may even expect friends of the author or clients of the publishers to provide glowing testimonials. We take these accolades with a large grain of salt.

But numbers aren't supposed to lie, and if a book is popular, we might reasonably conclude that it is worth our time and money. Creating a false impression of popularity is therefore an act of thievery, even if it may not be punishable in court.

As for Benny, since he did nothing wrong, and since he believes that his book offers genuine value to its readers, he shares none of the bookseller's guilt. However, he should insist that the bookseller discontinue the practice, or go find another shop to sell his book.

No One Here but Us Chickens

Daniel, who owned a neighborhood restaurant, received a call from his friend Michael, who owned a local catering business. Michael's freezer had broken down just as he received a shipment of frozen chickens. He asked if he could store his chickens in Daniel's freezer for a couple of weeks until he got his own freezer repaired.

Daniel had room to spare and was happy to help Michael out. When Michael arrived with the chickens, Daniel noticed that the expiration date on the cartons was past due. He pointed this out to Michael, who shrugged it off.

"The expiration date only applies when they're fresh," he said. "Once they're frozen, you can keep them forever."

Daniel wasn't so sure, but it was Michael's business, so he let the matter drop.

A month passed, and Daniel heard nothing from Michael. He called Michael, who apologized and said he'd be by that week to get his chickens.

More weeks went by, with Michael making excuses every time Daniel called to ask him to retrieve his chickens.

One afternoon, Daniel got a call from a nearby restaurateur. "The inspectors are making surprise visits this week," he told Daniel. "They've already dropped in on me and they could be at your place any moment. Make sure you have everything in order."

Daniel remembered the expiration date on Michael's chickens. It had been 3 months since Michael had dropped them off "for a couple of weeks." Daniel was mildly annoyed about the chickens taking up freezer space for so long, but now they actually threatened his livelihood. If the inspectors saw the expiration dates, they might not agree with Michael's reasoning and might not believe that Daniel was storing them for someone else. They might fine him, or even shut him down.

Daniel decided he had given Michael enough chances. He carried the chicken cases into the back alley and tossed them into his Dumpster.

Two hours later, Michael showed up. "I'm here for my chickens," he said with a smile.

Daniel explained why he hadn't been able to hold Michael's chickens any longer, saying he was free to retrieve them from the Dumpster. However, in the summer heat the chickens had defrosted enough to attract some local cats, which had rendered the chickens unfit for humans.

Michael demanded that Daniel compensate him for the chickens. Daniel replied that he had ceased to be responsible when Michael failed to retrieve his chickens on time.[4]

Grapple with the Gray

List two or three reasons supporting Michael's claim against Daniel.

List two or three reasons exonerating Daniel from damages.

Did Daniel have another alternative?

Having weighed the options, what would you have done if you were Daniel?

---

[4]Adapted from Y. Zilberstein. 2013. Veha'arev Na (Jerusalem, Israel: Philipp Feldheim).

Gray Matters

There's no question that Michael exploited Daniel's kindness by failing to pick up his chickens at the agreed time. If he legitimately intended to leave them only 2 weeks and ran into unexpected delays, he should have explained his circumstances to Daniel and asked for an extension. After a reasonable grace period, and having received no reasonable excuse, Daniel had every right to issue an ultimatum.

When he accepted responsibility for the chickens, Daniel simultaneously accepted responsibility to look after the chickens as if they were his own. This required him to ensure that the freezer remained in working condition and take reasonable precautions against theft. Once the originally agreed-upon time period elapsed, however, responsibility reverted to Michael to pick up his chickens or formally renew his arrangement with Daniel. Since Michael failed to do so, Daniel is no longer responsible for the chickens.

The question here, however, is whether or not Daniel had the right to actively cause Michael a financial loss by disposing of the chickens. And even if he did, was he obligated to inform Michael that he was doing so, and perhaps give him a reasonable deadline before taking action?

Under normal circumstances, that would be so. The added wrinkle here is that the possible arrival of health inspectors at any moment posed an imminent threat of harm to Daniel's business. If I agree to carry your case of gold bullion across the Atlantic, my responsibility ends if my ship sinks and I have to swim for my life. Here, too, the possibility of inspectors arriving at any moment left Daniel with no option other than removing the chickens from his freezer rather than risk significant financial loss.

Nevertheless, it would have been proper to call Michael immediately to inform him that his chickens were being left in the alley. Michael's previous unresponsiveness does not exempt Daniel from making an effort to give him fair warning.

Daniel might also have attempted a more creative solution, like putting the chickens in his car and letting Michael know that he had until the end of the day to retrieve them or they would be disposed of.

In a similar situation, where one merchant stored his furniture in another merchant's warehouse and failed to remove it, the Jewish legal authority Rabbi Moshe Feinstein ruled that even though the space might be needed for inventory, the warehouse owner was not permitted to dispose of the furniture or leave it vulnerable to theft or vandalism. He advised the warehouse owner to find another storage facility and move the furniture there, allowing him to sell as much as was necessary to cover the cost of transport and continued storage.

It's All About You

In 1997, a study by the University of Leicester found that when supermarkets played background music in the store aisles, customers were 70 percent more likely to buy German wine when German music was playing and French wine when French music was playing.

This is just one of many psychological tricks used to influence sales. Products are often placed between lower- and higher-priced alternatives to convince shoppers they are getting better quality at less cost. Stores typically play relaxing music that encourages customers to take their time. Most stores don't have clocks in visible locations, and grocery stores notoriously rearrange how they shelve their products every 2 years so customers have to hunt for what they want and, along the way, find themselves tempted by products they had no intention of buying.

Color schemes, background images, and font selection all influence our subconscious minds. According to the Society for Consumer Psychology, merely composing advertising copy with words in alphabetical order appeals to our subconscious desire to find patterns in life and makes products seem more attractive.[5]

Of course, the familiar phenomenon of celebrity endorsement thrives on the absurd equation between product quality and famous spokespeople.

Then there are rebates. Marketers know that customers mail in their rebate coupons less than 50 percent of the time.

Although there is no deception or overt manipulation, is it unethical to take advantage of psychological nature to influence customer buying habits?

Grapple with the Gray

List two or three reasons why these marketing practices are acceptable.
List two or three reasons why these marketing practices are unacceptable.
Is there another alternative?
Having weighed the options as a marketer, what would you do?

---

[5]Science Daily. 2019. "True Lies: How Letter Patterns Color Perceptions of Truth." www.sciencedaily.com/releases/2019/09/190925113002.htm.

Gray Matters

We're all familiar with the principle of *caveat emptor*—let the buyer beware. This does not give free license to sellers to engage in fraud, but it does place the burden of due diligence upon buyers to investigate purchases before concluding their transactions.

Perhaps the most relevant application of *caveat emptor* relates to the field of advertising. Marketing is, by definition, the art of manipulation. A clever jingle that sticks in our minds, a sincere-sounding actor assuring us of the benefits of a product, a slew of superlatives and promises—all of these are designed to convince us to part with our money in pursuit of happiness.

As humorist Will Rogers quipped in the 1931 movie *A Connecticut Yankee*, "advertising makes you spend money you haven't got for things that you don't want."

However, the ethics of advertising may have less to do with marketing techniques than with the quality of the product. Sometimes buyers are reluctant to spend money on products or services that will provide them with genuine benefit; sometimes they need to be lured away from inferior products made attractive by clever ad campaigns.

In modern business parlance, consultants urge marketers to *pull* prospective clients and consumers toward a sale rather than attempt to *push* them into it. By attractively offering a product or service of demonstrable quality and value at a fair price, an ethical vendor can make it easier for consumers to make decisions that will ultimately serve their own best interests.

The ethics of marketing, therefore, have much to do with intent: marketing with the intent to provide quality service is persuasion; marketing with the intent to exploit is manipulation. Using marketing techniques to help buyers make choices that are truly to their advantage can be interpreted as an act of charity and kindness, but only if it's authentically done in the buyer's best interest.

Commuting Sentences

Imagine that you're an Uber driver. You wake up early to catch the morning commuter crowd, only to find on your phone an updated, 27-page, single-spaced Technology Services Agreement. Without agreeing to the terms, you can't use the app. Without the app, you can't make your living.

Chances are, you'll press "I agree." The app makes it even easier by allowing you to agree without opening the document.

Uber drivers don't have to imagine this scenario. Among the many provisions included in the update of November 25, 2019, were clauses requiring drivers to settle disputes through a private arbitration company paid by Uber and prohibiting them from joining class-action lawsuits. Buried in the legalese, where few drivers would find it, was an opt-out clause to the arbitration provision.

If they pressed the "I agree" button, drivers still had 30 days to opt out. But this only helped if they knew what they clicked, why it might be in their interests to opt out, and that they had the option to do so.

Uber fought the opt-out clause in court and lost. In an effort to make the process more difficult, the company argued in open court that creating a designated e-mail address for opting out was too technically difficult to implement and therefore imposed *on the company* an unreasonable burden.

Grapple with the Gray
    List two or three reasons defending Uber's policy.
    List two or three reasons against Uber's policy.
    Is there another alternative for either the company or the drivers?
    Having weighed the options, what would you do if you were an Uber driver?

Gray Matters

In some cases, it's hard to see both sides of an issue. Companies and corporations have long been accused of favoring arbitration, both because they can choose the arbiter and because they can minimize negative publicity.

To the extent this may be true, it becomes a classic case study in ethics. Most of us click user agreements without reading them carefully—assuming we read them at all. In many cases, the stakes are small, so we don't worry. But as potential risks increase, so does our responsibility to know what rights we may be giving away when we sign or click.

Companies know that we don't have adequate time, inclination, or legal understanding, and they take full advantage of that knowledge. In the case of Uber, sending out the updated agreement early in the morning merely compounded injury with insult, forcing drivers to choose due diligence at the expense of doing their jobs. Consciously making it difficult to opt out is indisputably an act of bad faith.

Uber is a brilliant business model that should benefit all parties and provide the ultimate win–win. It's disheartening to see a company looking for an opportunity to take advantage of drivers without whom it could not function.

Moreover, as a commuting consumer, what is one to do? To boycott Uber for unfair practices toward drivers harms the drivers themselves. There's also the complication of urban taxi drivers who paid a small fortune for their licenses, only to be undercut by the tech upstart. Should our concern for them motivate us to forgo the convenience of Uber and pay their higher rates? When should government regulators intervene to protect established entrepreneurs from the inevitable alliance of technology and free enterprise against which they have no way to fight back?

When a culture is built on principles of ethics, these kinds of thorny questions will be addressed at the outset rather than fought over in court after the fact. Creative solutions are often available. But they rarely emerge from legal combat, and never from thinly disguised efforts to manipulate circumstances in our favor at the expense of others.

Strolling Along

You come home with your new baby stroller that you bought for $350. You've just opened the box and taken out the stroller when you find a promotional offer in the mail—the exact same stroller is on sale at a competing store for $300.

You call up the manager of the first store and explain what happened. "If I had seen the ad first," you explain, "I would have bought the stroller from your competitor. I think it would be fair if you gave me a $50 refund."

The manager replies, "Listen, stores have sales and specials all the time. The price is the price. You're certainly welcome to return the stroller for a refund, but that's all I can do for you."

You hang up the phone and start making a mental calculation. You'll have to take time to pack up the stroller, drive to the store, spend time on the paperwork getting your refund, go to the other store, and go through the buying process all over again there. You decide that the $50 just isn't worth it.

The next moment, the phone rings. It's the manager of the store. "Listen," he says, "I was thinking about your call, and I decided that you're right. We appreciate your business, and we want you to feel good about your purchase. Come back in at your convenience, and I'll be happy to refund $50 from the price."

Since you've already made up your mind that you accept the price you paid and have no intention of returning the stroller, are you entitled to take the refund?[6]

Grapple with the Gray

    List two or three reasons in favor of claiming the refund.
    List two or three reasons not to take it.
    Is there another option?
    Having weighed the options, what would you do?

---

[6]Adapted from Y. Zilberstein. 2013. *Veha'arev Na* (Jerusalem, Israel: Philipp Feldheim).

Gray Matters

Many stores today offer a price guarantee. Some even offer to double the difference if you find a cheaper price, either before or after you buy. It's also arguable that basic customer service mandates such policies.

Nevertheless, these policies are the prerogative of the shopkeeper, not the right of the customer. If you don't like the prices or the policies at any store, you are free to take your business elsewhere.

Of course, once the manager made the offer, it is the legal right of the customer to take advantage of it. The question here is not legal but moral. Once the customer made up his mind that he was at peace with the original price, is it ethical for him to claim a refund that was only offered after he expressed his discontent? Unlike the case of Rabbi Safra and the diamond, you never would have paid the higher price for the stroller in the first place if you knew you could buy it for less.

When this question was brought to Rabbi Yitzchok Zilberstein of Jerusalem, he suggested that the proper course of action would be to simply call up the manager, explain the series of events, and ask whether the manager would consider it proper for him to come in and claim the refund.

The wisdom of Rabbi Zilberstein's response provides a simple yet profound insight into the very nature of ethics. First, make an effort to understand the other party's point of view. Second, communicate clearly to avoid having to make assumptions. Those two simple steps will eliminate much of the gray areas that cloud our lives.

PART 3
Ethical Education

Sages, be careful with your words, lest you exile yourself to a place of evil waters, where the students who follow you will drink and die.
—Ethics of Fathers 1:11

Everyone Is above Average

Readers of a certain age will recall a time when academic grades reflected actual achievement, when sports awards recognized genuine athletic prowess, and when most young people contented themselves with residing outside the bright circle of popular acclaim.

But all that has changed. Where a grade of C used to stand for competent but uninspired work, it now stands in place of D or F, either of which is viewed as an academic nuclear button. Participation trophies are the norm in baseball and soccer, lest some children feel less accomplished than others—even if they are.

To make matters worse, instructors are under pressure to not only inflate students' grades but to write glowing recommendations, even if this forces their testimonials into the realm of fiction or fantasy. In a few celebrated cases, disgruntled students and parents filed lawsuits against instructors who dared to issue a grade the student actually earned.

Many instructors have given up the fight and acquiesced to the new normal. They simply don't believe it's worth subjecting themselves to angry calls, pressure from administrators, and the specter of litigation. But more than that, they may rationalize that grade inflation is necessary for those good but unexceptional students who will find themselves competing with other good but unexceptional students. If students from other schools enjoy the benefit of inflated grades and fancifully written recommendations, why should their own students appear lackluster because they were honestly evaluated?

What should a teacher do? Provide an honest assessment, or go with the flow of inflated grades and hyperbolic reference letters?

Grapple with the Gray

List two or three reasons for grading honestly.
List two or three reasons for inflating the grades.
Is there another alternative?
Having weighed the options, as a teacher what would you do?

Gray Matters

This problem offers a singular dilemma. Grade and recommendation inflation hurts everyone, particularly the student it supposes to help. Genuinely talented or hardworking students are not distinguished for their accomplishments above their mediocre peers. Weaker students may gain admission to programs which they are not equipped to succeed in. Selection staff lose the ability to differentiate between one student and another; consequently, they are unable to make informed admissions decisions.

However, once the problem exists, it hardly seems equitable that a few students should suffer at the hands of one honest evaluator while the majority benefit from a broken system.

Philosophically, any instructor who participates in grade and recommendation inflation is complicit in undermining standards of educational integrity. But again, philosophy will not help the unfortunate student who has the bad luck to draw an honest evaluator.

Perhaps a partial solution is for principled instructors to decline writing recommendations for any students about whom they are less than enthusiastic. No doubt, a student who is turned away by one teacher will find other teachers willing to substitute fact with fiction. This itself raises the more nuanced problem of encouraging students to shop around for whatever authority will enable them to manipulate the system.

More to the point, this solution won't help with grading. Teachers can decline to give grades to average students. Nevertheless, it's likely that any teacher who grades honestly across the board will acquire a reputation for tough standards. If the teacher's class is required, all students will be equally subject to those standards; if it is an elective, weaker students may elect not to take it.

As we've already seen, upholding ethical standards becomes more complicated when doing so comes at others' expense, particularly when those others are trapped in an unethical system. Even so, simply giving up on educational standards seems a poor option for those who commit their lives to preparing the next generation to be successful contributors to society.

Chilling Effects

In 2013, Disney released the animated film sensation *Frozen*, which went on to gross over a billion dollars in revenues. It was the story of Elsa who, after being locked away to protect others from magic powers she could not control, eventually fled the kingdom and sought the freedom of isolation where she could be herself.

The turning point for Elsa arrives as she climbs into the mountains and sings the popular song, "Let it Go." The lyrics include the following lines:

It's time to see what I can do,
To test the limits and break through.
No right, no wrong, no rules for me.
I'm free.

Let it go, let it go.
That perfect girl is gone.
Here I stand in the light of day.
Let the storm rage on.

Of course, in true Disney form, sister Anna journeys into the mountains to find Elsa, eventually convincing her to return to the kingdom and assume her place as queen.

Nevertheless, some critics have argued that the message contained in Elsa's anthem, "Let it Go," taken out of context from the movie, encourages children to reject conventional standards, rebel against social norms, and challenge parental and school authority.

A generation earlier, in 1979, the band Pink Floyd released its concept album *The Wall*, perhaps best known for these lyrics:

We don't need no education.
We don't need no thought control.
No dark sarcasm in the classroom.
Teachers—leave them kids alone.

The songwriter, Roger Waters, would later explain his composition as a critique of a system of standardized education that often allowed struggling students to fall through the cracks. But whatever his motives, reports followed the album's release of students breaking out in unison to disrupt classes with the cynical lyrics.

In the same way, many contemporary rap songs have been criticized for seeming to promote misogyny, cultural tribalism, and violence.

All of which leads us to this question:

To what degree do artists have a moral obligation to anticipate the effect their art will have on society, particularly on young children who may lack the sophistication to recognize satire and understand it in context?

Grapple with the Gray

- List two or three reasons why artists should focus solely on their art without concern for how it will be interpreted.
- List two or three reasons why artists should self-censor their art by anticipating its impact.
- Is there another alternative?
- Having weighed the options, what would you do as an artist?

Gray Matters

In 1729, Jonathan Swift published a short pamphlet titled, *A Modest Proposal: For preventing the children of poor people in Ireland from being a burden on their parents or country, and for making them beneficial to the publick.*

After briefly identifying the problem of unwanted, indigent children in Ireland, the author then outlines in dispassionate, clinical detail a solution whereby these children might be slaughtered and cooked to feed the remainder of the population. By advancing such a reasonable-sounding argument for such a shocking policy, the author effectively skewered the ruling classes who showed little inclination to address the plight of the poor.

Of course, the power of Swift's satire was that (almost) everyone knew it was satire. But imagine if some had interpreted his plan as a serious proposal and proposed its implementation.

Over time, shock value has become an end in itself for many artists. Despite—or perhaps, because of—their talent and creativity, many artists leave too much room for audiences of any age to misinterpret their meaning, even if we assume that their intentions were as noble and purely artistic as they might later claim.

Art is a form of communication and, as such, should communicate values that will elevate society, not accelerate its descent into chaos. As dark as George Orwell's dystopian classic *1984* may have been, it was clearly intended as a warning against the natural outcome of totalitarian government. Similarly, such modern classics as *The Matrix, The Giver*, and *Blade Runner* leave little room to misinterpret their moralizing.

You don't have to look too hard to recognize how television, cinema, and the Internet have recalibrated social norms throughout modern culture. Whether you believe those changes have been for better or for worse, the influence of art on contemporary values is undeniable.

In the words of Spiderman, *with great power comes great responsibility*. Artists have the same responsibility as politicians, entertainers, and anyone else who holds the spotlight to consider how their words, their actions, and their art will—or might—influence the society that consumes them.

Even for those of us who are not artists, don't we also share the ethical obligation to resist the darkness of cynicism and contribute to the light of hope for a better future and faith in the nobility of humankind?

The Grand Design

A noted psychologist had just finished his address to a group of professionals when a member of the audience approached him and introduced himself. The psychologist immediately recognized the name. Before him stood a world-famous doctor, once featured on the cover of *Time* magazine, whose medical innovations had transformed treatments and revolutionized curative procedures.

The esteemed doctor proceeded to confess that he had suffered his entire life from depression. As a boy, he loved to draw, and he had possessed a natural talent for artistic design. Growing up, he dreamt of one day becoming a successful architect.

But his parents had other ideas. "Architecture?" they asked. "No. You need to use your intelligence to support a family. You are going to medical school."

And so he did, with almost unparalleled success. Nonetheless, despite his extraordinary contributions to medicine, the doctor felt unfulfilled in life for not having pursued his passion.

Sometime later, the psychologist lamented the insistence of the doctor's parents, how they had deprived him of the life he had wanted and the sense of purpose that he had never realized. When he finished, the psychologist found himself confronted by several doctors from the audience.

"We know who you were talking about," they said. "Do you have any idea how many lives were saved through his procedures and inventions? How dare you suggest that his own personal gratification outweighs the contribution he made to the world and the people he benefited?"

The psychologist later expressed his ambivalence. Were those other doctors right? Was the cost of personal satisfaction outweighed by the value to society? He admitted that he did not have an answer himself.

Grapple with the Gray

    List two or three reasons supporting the psychologist's inclination that the parents failed their son.

List two or three reasons supporting the other doctors' assertion that
   the greater good outweighs the individual lack of fulfillment.
Is there another alternative?
Having weighed the options as a parent, what do you say?

Gray Matters

The doctors who criticized the psychologist are indulging in a common fallacy. Now that we know the outcome, it's easy to project back and opine what should or should not have been done at the beginning. However, Monday-morning-quarterbacking is useless when the first whistle signals the opening kickoff on Sunday afternoon.

If the parents had a crystal ball and could see alternative futures—one where their son lived a highly influential but ultimately unfulfilled life, and another where he enjoyed personal satisfaction but left no great mark upon society—then we might be able to engage in a reasonable debate. Indeed, self-sacrifice on any level for the greater good is a value that supersedes almost every other.

But to force a child to abandon not only his hopes and dreams but his natural talents and passions is an entirely different matter. Moreover, the parents here were not committed to all the good their son might do as a doctor but rather the financial rewards they saw in his professional future. Not every doctor changes the medical landscape for the better. Indeed, some do great harm. And some architects truly do change the world for the better through their visionary achievements. Imagine if Frank Lloyd Wright had become a radiologist and Frank Gehry a thoracic surgeon.

Of course, fiscal reality must figure into any deliberation of vocational future. A child determined to become a poet needs to be made aware of the very long odds of supporting himself, just as a child set on becoming a major-league pitcher or NBA center is best served to have some kind of backup plan to ensure financial security.

But to disregard a child's dreams and inclinations out of hand, especially in our current age of opportunity, no matter how practical or idealistic the motives, seems both insensitive and cruel.

The Other Foot

In October 2019, a federal judge upheld the right of Harvard University to set a higher standard of admissions criteria for Asian-American students and allow entry to a larger number of underrepresented ethnicities, thereby creating a more diverse student population.

The case hearkened all the way back to the 1978 Bakke decision, which declared racial quotas unconstitutional while maintaining the constitutionality of affirmative action.

On the one hand, there is clear benefit to creating an academic environment in which a diversity of cultures, values, and viewpoints are represented. A variegated student body promotes discussion and debate in a way that a homogeneous community cannot.

But on the other hand, it seems unfair that a university—or any organization—should have one set of standards for one group and a different set of standards for others. Is that not essentially the same kind of discrimination that made the need arise for affirmative action in the first place?

Grapple with the Gray
    List two or three reasons in favor of including ethnic criteria in college admissions.
    List two or three reasons why colleges should not consider ethnicity.
    Is there another alternative?
    Having weighed the options, how would you structure college admissions practices?

Gray Matters

We should be able to agree on two points of fact. First, universities face a problem in providing a diverse environment when some ethnicities, as a group, achieve above the curve and others below the curve. Second, not every problem has a simple solution.

Returning to the Bakke case, the question there addressed reserving a set number of spaces for certain minority students, thereby effectively shutting out candidates who were otherwise qualified for admission.

The challenge to the quota system extended beyond simple unfairness. To fill quotas, universities sometimes had to relax standards to the point of accepting candidates who were not merely *less* qualified but *under*-qualified. This led to a disproportionate number of dropouts, which rendered pointless the exclusion of qualified students by failing to provide the students who took their places a realistic pathway for success.

The Harvard case appears more nuanced, adding points as it were to the resumes of otherwise qualified students based on ethnic identity. One might reasonably argue that, in a case where two candidates were identical according to every other metric, race or identity might be used to break the tie. But to penalize one student for an accident of birth that has no bearing on academic performance in order to achieve an abstract ideal of diversity seems inequitable.

That abstract ideal, however, has practical ramifications. In a very real sense, the educational experience of every student is enhanced by a diverse school environment. To achieve that diversity, more qualified students whose admission would contribute to a less diverse studentry must be turned away.

This is not fair. But it may be just, in the sense that it advances sound education principles that are foundational to the existence of the university. Not everyone can be served, and the students who find themselves excluded because of race are the collateral damage of an imperfect system trying to make the best of an imperfect situation.

What can make this inequity palatable, however, is the perception of consistency and genuine good intention.

This is where many colleges and universities fall short, undermining their own credibility by failing to show consistent application of the values they espouse.

A college campus is meant to provide a marketplace of ideas, a place for spirited debate and intellectual experimentation, an incubator for young minds to develop by questioning, challenging, and investigating, as well as having their own ideas challenged and having to defend their points of view.

In recent years, however, many colleges have become caricatures of political correctness as they've become overtaken by groupthink. Instead of providing safe spaces for free-flowing dialogue, the term "safe space" has been hijacked to mean a place where feelings and sensitivities are protected from even the most reasonable and objective ideas lest they cause offense or discomfort.

This trend has increasingly turned colleges into the antithesis of what they were meant to be, shutting down dialogue and demanding intellectual conformity. Diversity of identity has been offset by homogeneity of thought—precisely the opposite of what Harvard claimed in its diversity defense.

The acid test for ethics is whether or not attitudes and actions are applied equally to each side of the ideological divide. By claiming the moral high ground over ethnic diversity while suppressing intellectual diversity, universities should expect that marginalized students will become even more militant as they perceive *equity* as a smokescreen to conceal reverse racism.

Yearning to Be Free

Imagine that your child comes home with the following homework assignment:

"You own a plantation or farm and therefore need more workers. You begin to get more involved in the slave trade industry and have slaves work on your farm. Your product to trade is slaves. These could be worth a lot."

Parents of fifth graders in suburban St. Louis didn't have to imagine. The social studies assignment brought home by their children included a blank line for students to set a price per slave.

Predictably, news of the assignment exploded across the Internet, making national headlines and eliciting cries of cultural insensitivity. In short order, the teacher was placed on administrative leave.

Perhaps the teacher merely meant to be historically accurate in teaching the economics of plantation society. I would like to think that the teacher hoped to instill in students an appreciation for the evils of a slave culture that equated human beings with chattel. Either way, the teacher clearly failed to anticipate the reaction provoked by the assignment.

Grapple with the Gray

- List two or three reasons why the teacher deserved to be suspended.
- List two or three reasons why suspension might have been an overreaction.
- Could the teacher have included slave trading into the assignment in a more sensitive way?
- Having weighed the options, how would you, as principal, have responded to the assignment?

Gray Matters

The demographic of the school system in which the incident occurred is about as homogenous as imaginable—ethnically, religiously, and economically. Without exposure to people from other cultures, it's virtually impossible to avoid stereotyping, bias and, in this case, an inability to anticipate when offense might be taken.

The most unfortunate part of this story is the missed opportunity. How powerful a lesson might it have been had the teacher instructed the students to imagine that they were slaves, that they could be bought and sold as property, separated from their families, deprived of self-determination and the basic rights and comforts that they take for granted?

Of course, whether or not such an assignment would be age-appropriate for fifth graders adds another layer to the discussion. Presenting school children with content beyond their level of intellectual ability and sophistication is always a recipe for failure, no matter how creatively packaged.

At some point in their educational careers, however, young people need exposure to the wider world. Without it, they eventually become unwilling contributors to the perpetuation of small-mindedness and unconscious prejudice.

Children who aren't exposed to different cultures don't have the opportunity to acquire a broad worldview or develop an understanding of cultural differences. When they grow into adults, they aren't able to impart cultural sensitivity to their children or their students. This may not be their fault, but it is everyone's responsibility to correct.

Well-intentioned people do not deserve to be punished because they were never taught to be sensitive. But every one of us has a responsibility to expand our awareness, to find mentors to teach us what we don't know that we don't know.

We've all learned about the famous road that's paved with good intentions. Part of being ethical is being curious, being willing to seek out knowledge that may not seem immediately relevant to our lives. Curiosity requires vulnerability, admitting ignorance or a lack of understanding.

This is why the sages taught that a timid person will never become wise. If we are afraid to become students of life and the world around us, we will never acquire the worldly awareness that enables us to live lives of genuine integrity.

PART 4
Ethical Society

The intemperate despise a person of moral integrity; under the guise of honesty, they seek his soul.
—Proverbs 29:10

Behind Drawer #1

In September 2013, Rabbi Noah Muroff brought home an ordinary office desk he had bought on Craigslist. Finding the desk an inch too wide to fit through his office doorway, the high school teacher from New Haven, Connecticut, got out his screwdriver, removed the desktop, and discovered a plastic bag stuffed in the space behind the drawers. The bag contained $98,000 in cash.

He knew that the money must belong to the previous owner, an elderly lady who told him she had bought the desk from Staples and put it together herself.

Was he obligated to return the money?

Grapple with the Gray

List two or three reasons for keeping the money.
List two or three reasons for returning it to the previous owner.
Is there another option?
Having weighed the options, what would you do?

Gray Matters

Obviously, the previous owner had forgotten about the $98,000 altogether. This allows for a certain rationale that once a person has forgotten that they ever owned an object or money, they have effectively lost hope of ever getting it back. At that point, the money or property might be justifiably considered ownerless.

This justification, however, is relevant when applied to obligation as a finder to search for an unknown owner. The responsibility a finder has to publicize the discovery of lost property diminishes in proportion to both the impracticality of identifying a legitimate owner and the owner's likely expectation that the property is gone for good.

However, when you know with certainty the identity of the previous owner, ethics requires you to make every reasonable effort to return it.

And that's what Rabbi Muroff did, bringing his children along to teach them the lesson of integrity. Needless to say, the former owner of the desk was as grateful as she was astonished.

If the hidden bag had contained a family heirloom, a private letter, or an old photo album, this story never would have made headlines. Having the name and contact information of the owner, most of us would not think twice about returning an object of sentimental value that is worth nothing to us.

That's exactly the point. There is still some modest accomplishment in acting ethically when the stakes are low. The real challenge comes the moment self-interest kicks in, and the challenge grows stronger the more we can tick off sound reasons to support acting in our own self-interest.

A wise person once said: "You will never have any shortage of *legitimate* excuses for not doing what you ought to do." Whether the temptation or the effort is great or small, whether a hundred dollars or a hundred thousand, the principles of ethics remain the same. Acting with moral consistency is the hallmark of a truly ethical person.

Share the Wealth

On the Jewish festival of Chanukah, many favor pure olive oil over wax candles to kindle the lights of the menorah during the 8 days of the holiday.

In some synagogues, particularly in Israel, it is common to find members of the congregation selling bottles of oil for the convenience of the parishioners. Often, the oil is left in the vestibule or foyer along with an envelope for cash or check payments. Transactions are on the honor system.

Imagine that on one occasion, a man arrives early to find a case of 20 bottles marked at 19 shekels each. Suddenly he has an inspiration. He makes a quick mental calculation, takes one bottle, then rewrites the note to indicate a price of 20 shekels.

He reasons that the seller of the oil will make 380 shekels once the bottles sell out either way. Furthermore, as long as the buyers are willing to pay 20 shekels for a bottle, he isn't stealing. He concludes that he isn't hurting anyone, and he walks off with his "free" bottle of oil.

The man is so impressed with himself that, when he gets home, he brags to his wife about what he did.

His wife is less impressed. "Are you out of your mind?" she says. "You can't do that!"

Which of them is right?[1]

Grapple with the Gray
    List two or three reasons in defense of the husband.
    List two or three reasons in defense of the wife.
    Is there another option?
    Having weighed the options, what would you do?

---

[1] Adapted from Y. Zilberstein. 2013. *Veha'arev Na* (Jerusalem, Israel: Philipp Feldheim).

Gray Matters

The husband assumes that, since no one loses, his gimmick must be okay. The first problem with his reasoning is that others actually are losing—the other 19 buyers are each overpaying by 5 percent for their oil, even if they don't know it.

The second problem is much worse: Legitimizing an act of embezzlement undermines both the letter and the spirit of the law.

As we've already seen, the more people seek to manipulate and pervert the system for their own personal benefit, the more likely the system is to break down. A community flourishes and endures only by virtue of a universally recognized social contract that values the qualities of good citizenry. If all that motivates us is the fear of getting caught, inevitably we will all become criminals by attempting to fly under the radar whenever self-interest and opportunism coincide.

What's remarkable in this story is how proud the husband is of his chicanery. Never for a moment did he wrestle with his conscience; not for one instant did it occur to him that he was doing anything wrong.

This is why it's critical that we surround ourselves with people of sound moral character, and why we need to consult with objective parties before we jump at opportunities to profit at others' expense.

How fortunate for the husband that his wife saw the situation more clearly, and that she wasn't afraid to tell him what he needed to hear. How unfortunate for him that he didn't think to ask her opinion before he acted.

In this case, the husband created two additional problems for himself. First, he has no way to return the stolen money to his victims, since he doesn't know who they are. Second, he may not even have fulfilled his obligation to kindle the Chanukah lights, since the use of stolen oil invalidates the ritual.

By the Book?

True story:

Susan was working in the back office of a neighborhood clinic one morning, when a patient arrived and was admitted for consultation. Susan heard raised voices, after which the patient reappeared and quickly left the clinic in a state of apparent grief or anger. Had there been some disagreement or misunderstanding? Susan assumed so but couldn't know for sure.

Under normal circumstances, Susan probably wouldn't have thought twice. But only a week earlier, a disgruntled client had left an office just down the street after a conflict, then returned with a gun and started shooting.

Susan didn't want to take the chance that her inaction might put others (and herself) at risk. Perhaps with a simple check-in she might determine if there was any cause for genuine concern.

Because all visits were confidential, looking up the man's identity would be a violation of privacy. Susan tried to reach her supervisor for permission to open the database, but her supervisor was unavailable.

Susan took the initiative. She looked up the man's name and phone number, then gave him a call.

"Hello," she said into the phone. "I'm calling to check in … you seemed upset when you left our office. Is there anything I can do to help?"

"Oh, no," the man replied. "I was a little distressed, but I'm fine now. Thanks so much for calling."

Subsequently, Susan found herself reprimanded by her supervisor.

Was she wrong to do what she did?

Grapple with the Gray

List two or three reasons in favor of what Susan did.
List two or three reasons why Susan was wrong.
Is there another option?
Having weighed the options, what should Susan have done?

Gray Matters

There are a lot of layers to this scenario.

Imagine if Susan chose to respect the client's confidentiality, and an hour later he returned with a gun and opened fire. Would Susan be considered negligent or culpable for failing to follow up? Is she morally obligated to risk losing her job if she believes loss to life is a real possibility? Does her own personal conscience give her the right to break the law?

Does suspicion or intuited concern ever override personal privacy?

This same debate continues to rage on a national level with respect to the Patriot Act and personal privacy laws. The government needs access to personal information to protect the public. It may need to suspend the rights of individuals to protect public safety in large numbers.

How do we balance the general welfare against the rights of the individual? How do we ensure that the government will not abuse the power we give it for our own protection? If some of us would rather relinquish a measure of privacy for enhanced security, while others accept the security risks that come with greater privacy protection, how do we, as a society, resolve the disparity of opinions? Indeed, the more we accept the wisdom of "see something, say something," the more we implicitly recognize that sometimes collective security must trump the individual's right to privacy.

There are no simple solutions to the conflict of ethical interests. Only by continuously refining and recalibrating our collective moral compass can we approach these dilemmas with reason and integrity so that, time after time, we can get as close as possible to making sound ethical decisions.

But abstract ethical questions would not have helped Susan that day. She had to make a decision, she had to make it on her own, and she had to make it in the moment. She opted to take action, to put safety ahead of regulations and ahead of her own job security. She weighed the potential costs and benefits, then acted according to her conscience.

Indeed, the greatest ethical violation may have been the system itself, which made it necessary for Susan to break the law in order to do the right thing. She may have been legally in the wrong; but there is little doubt that she was ethically in the right.

In fact, the ethical courage Susan demonstrated offers an additional insight into ethical decision making. Sometimes we need to be prepared to accept the consequences of acting right at the hands of others who won't recognize the rightness of our actions.

Seeds of Doubt

A CEO calls together her executive team and says to them:

"I've decided that I need a chief executive adviser, a strong right hand, a confidant, someone I can absolutely trust to help me run this company. And I've devised an innovative way to choose this person."

She then hands out to each executive a little bag and says, "In your bag you will find some seeds. I want you to take these seeds home and plant them. In 3 months, I'm going to ask you to bring in what you've grown from these seeds. Based on your results, I'm going to choose my chief adviser."

The executives wonder among themselves if the boss has gone a little batty. But she's the boss and, hey, this is a great opportunity.

Among the candidates is one junior executive who, no matter how hard he works, never seems to get the recognition he deserves. Now he sees his big chance. He goes home, goes online, and gathers all the information he can. He hurries to the local nursery and picks out the right pot, the right soil, the right fertilizer. He comes home, puts everything together, places the pot in exactly the right place for light and temperature. Then he sits back to wait.

Nothing happens. Nothing appears from the soil, not even one measly little shoot.

Back in the office, over the next days and weeks, all the executives are talking about how their plants are beginning to sprout, how they're getting big and beautiful and green and luscious.

The junior executive goes back online, goes back to the nursery, changes things around. Nothing works.

After 3 months, the big day arrives, and the executives bring in their potted plants, each one more beautiful and lusher than the next. And our poor executive comes in carrying a pot of dirt. He feels humiliated. The other executives are giving him looks, snickering, and making snide comments.

Throughout the day, the CEO makes her rounds. She stops at his desk, looks at his pot of dirt, makes a note on her tablet, then moves on. He's crestfallen. Opportunity lost.

At the end of the afternoon, the CEO gathers her executives together. "This has been a very instructive exercise," she says. "I want to tell you, that before I handed out the seeds, I took the whole bunch of them, put them in a vat of water, and boiled them. Now, it's remarkable how many of you were able to grow healthy plants from dead seeds!"

"Only one person in this office followed my instructions without resorting to deception, even though it appeared that he was sure to fail. That's the person I want as my chief adviser."

Grapple with the Gray
List two or three reasons why the CEO acted ethically.
List two or three reasons why the CEO acted unethically.
Is there another option?
Having weighed the options, should the CEO have done what she did?

Gray Matters

The first point to observe is that the CEO never actually lied. She simply withheld information and allowed her executives to draw their own conclusions. But adherence to literal truth doesn't let her off the hook. Indeed, some of the most effective lies are those that mislead without openly departing from the facts.

So was her deception justifiable? Perhaps.

It's interesting to observe that the closest friends of celebrities, athletes, and millionaires are often the same friends they had when they were just ordinary people. The reason is obvious: They don't have to worry that their old friends like them only for their newly acquired wealth or fame.

The same principle might apply here as well.

In a corporate culture, it's often difficult to tell who the sincere team players are and who are the artful opportunists playing whatever part they believe will advance their own position. A good leader knows that a willingness to fail is critical to a mindset of success, and honest, thoughtful criticism is an essential quality in an adviser.

Ironically, it's arguable that the CEO needed to resort to subterfuge in order to get to the truth, weeding out those executives likely to tell her only what they thought she wanted to hear. As it turned out, only one member of her team showed himself trustworthy enough to deserve the job.

Perhaps there is another benefit to her pretense. In the process, she may have taught her team a few lessons: Don't try to deceive me. Don't try to game the system. Don't give me the answer you think I want; tell me the truth.

Did the benefit of discovering and teaching truthfulness outweigh her passive deception? There's room to argue either way. As we will continue to see, grappling with ethical questions doesn't always bring us to a clear answer. But the grappling itself makes us more sensitive to the nuances of right and wrong. Every time we struggle toward moral clarity, we make ourselves better equipped to tackle the next moral challenge that comes along.

The Coin of the Realm

For decades, the United States Treasury Department and the U.S. mint have been trying to get Americans to use one-dollar coins in place of one-dollar bills. It costs twice as much to mint a dollar coin as to print a bill, but the coins last 15 times longer. The economic advantages are self-evident.

The British love their one-pound coins. But for some reason, Americans don't want to give up their bills. So when the treasury introduced the George Washington one-dollar coin in 2007, they offered an incentive program, making it possible to go online and order a roll of coins—40 coins for 40 dollars—and pay for them by credit card. The coins would arrive postage-free and easily make their way into circulation.

At first it seemed that the program was a success. The sale of coins was robust; in fact, it was a little too robust, as some people ordered thousands of dollars' worth of coins. Then, as soon as their coins arrived, these clever folks took them straight to the bank, sometimes in their original packaging, and deposited them directly into their accounts—pocketing the credit card points they got from buying them. The government ended up paying for a lot of postage and didn't get very many coins into circulation.

Grapple with the Gray
    List two or three reasons in favor of using the coins to get points.
    List two or three reasons against using the coins to get points.
    Is there another option?
    Having weighed the options, what would you do?

Gray Matters

When questioned about their manipulation of the government offer, many acquitted themselves by arguing that *it wasn't illegal*. This, of course, misses the point entirely. Although there was no contract or statement of conditions, the intent of the offer was clear—to get coins into circulation. By merely depositing them, these individuals violated the implicit terms of the deal.

Someone had to pay for all that postage. That someone is the government, which means that American tax dollars went to, among others, the person who bragged that he collected enough points buying coins to pay for his trip to Tahiti.

Do you want to pay for this charlatan's trip to Tahiti? I know I don't.

The problem here is, again, the conflation of what's legal with what's ethical. The moment we forget the difference between the two is the moment we find our moral compass spinning in all directions.

This is the reason why compliance laws by themselves are not only inadequate but often counterproductive. No law has been written that can't be circumvented through loopholes left by the impossibility of covering every contingency or anticipating every situation. Because loopholes, by definition, ignore the intent behind the law, they can only be plugged by a mindset that recognizes the spirit of the law as inseparable from the letter of the law.

"It's not illegal" is the last refuge of the unethical.

Dressed to Distress

In March 2017, United Airlines set off the first of many public relations firestorms when it refused to board a pair of teenage girls dressed in leggings. The girls' attire, it seems, was not in line with United's passenger dress code.

Not surprisingly, the decision set off a barrage of criticism across the Twittersphere. Many found the dress code sexist, others questioned whether it should apply to children, and still others thought it arbitrary, ill-defined, and inconsistently applied.

United responded by clarifying that, as family of employees, the girls were traveling on free passes and were therefore subject to the same dress code as those employees themselves would be if they were using the passes. Presumably, the intent behind the rule is to preserve a certain standard of decorum on every flight. Since the girls were not in compliance with the employee and family dress code, the gate agent followed protocol by refusing to let them board.

Grapple with the Gray
- List two or three reasons why United was correct to turn back the girls.
- List two or three reasons why United was wrong to turn back the girls.
- Were there any other options?
- Having weighed the options, what would you have done if you were the gate agent?

Gray Matters

Fashions change, and so do standards. When John F. Kennedy attended his presidential inauguration without a hat, instantaneously hats fell out of style. During the Civil War, women were not permitted to approach the army camps since the men occasionally came out of their tents without putting on their waistcoats. Female attire that's perfectly acceptable today could have landed a woman in jail a century ago.

But there's a difference between styles and standards. A relaxed dress code may work in the offices of Facebook and Google, but conventional businesses have discovered that productivity drops off when executives trade their button-down shirts and slacks for jeans and T-shirts.

Indeed, University of Hertfordshire psychology professor Karen Fine explains, "Professional work attire primes the brain to behave in ways consistent with that meaning." To a large degree, we are what we wear.

Nevertheless, any dress code invites trouble by resorting to ambiguous prohibitions against clothing that is "inappropriate" or "vulgar" while requiring the observance of "decency laws and community standards."

The charge of discrimination against women raises several issues. While it's certainly possible for men to wear clothing that is sexually suggestive, the opportunities are both less common and less diverse. Even the most flamboyant males are far less likely than women to be seen in public wearing spandex, plunging necklines, bare midriffs, or short shorts. In other words, the policy's emphasis on female attire is largely a response to the nature of contemporary fashion and the configuration of the human body.

The ambiguity over defining decency reflects the larger crisis in cultural values we face today. There once was a time when society agreed on what was decent and what was not, when social norms could be relied on to govern public behavior. And although many of those social strictures may have seemed arbitrary or contrived, they did contribute to a general attitude that an individual's public persona needs to project a measure of respect and dignity, and that every citizen bears an equal responsibility to contribute to the general maintenance of civil society.

In such times, common sense was enough to administer loosely worded regulations. When popular air travel was introduced in the 1950s, passengers dressed up in their finest attire to fly. It was considered a privilege, one carrying with it a duty to show appreciation and respect for the institution. In an age that worships unrestricted personal freedom, every loophole must be anticipated, which makes a mockery of regulations and makes enforcement a nightmare.

So if United Airlines wants to hold its employees to a more formal standard of attire when they're flying as a corporate perk, perhaps the company should be applauded for its professionalism. And if that requires family members who fly on nonrevenue tickets to spruce up a bit, is that such a high price to pay?

Shouldn't there be exceptions for children? Maybe. It does seem silly to ban pre-adolescents from wearing leggings to fly. Must there be consistency in enforcement? Of course. Arbitrary policing of rules is sometimes even worse than no rules at all.

That being said, perhaps it's not such a bad idea for us to be more conscious of our self-presentation, and less eager to discard the garments of dignity. Maybe then we would hold ourselves to a higher standard of behavior, and not be so quick to judge those who appreciate the value of self-censorship and the social graces.

Pay as You Go

Flying with children poses a variety of difficulties. Aside from the challenge of managing youthful squirreliness within the confines of a crowded passenger compartment, even booking the flight might not be simple. Airline policies change from time to time, and different companies have different rules.

Imagine this real-life scenario:

You're traveling across the Atlantic with your toddler. The airline you're flying charges 10 percent of the ticket price to hold the child in your lap. However, that deal is only available for children under two. Your child is 26 months, just over the limit, for which the airline requires you to buy the child her own seat for 90 percent of the full ticket price.

You know the child will spend virtually the entire trip in your lap regardless, so you see paying for a seat as a waste of money. However, you don't want to lie to the airline.

Your travel agent offers the following suggestion:

Buy the 10 percent ticket. Don't offer any information about your child's age. In all probability, the flight attendants will admit your family on the plane without question. If they ask your child's age, answer truthfully. If they tell you there is an age limit, apologize for your error and offer to pay for the seat.

Grapple with the Gray
List two or three reasons in favor of following the agent's advice.
List two or three reasons why you should not buy the cheaper ticket.
Is there another option?
Having weighed the options, what would you do?

Gray Matters

Airlines, like any business or service, have the right to impose whatever rules or charges they choose. As a patron, you have the privilege to take your business elsewhere. What you don't have the right to do knowingly defraud the airline.

Granted, "defraud" may be a bit too strong here—but only a bit. You are being consciously deceptive even as you skirt the edge of outright dishonesty. Ultimately, you will do more damage by far to your own ethical psyche than you will save in dollars and cents.

It was for this reason that Rabbi Yaakov Kaminetzky responded to this same question by answering, "It's not forbidden; but don't do it."

Once again, we find that any compromise of integrity brings us closer to the edge of the proverbial slippery slope—or pushes us entirely over the brink. The sages teach that the first time a person commits a transgression, it's a transgression. The second time, it's permitted. The third time, it's an act of virtue.

The more we rationalize improper behavior, the more automatically we accept improper behavior as appropriate, and the more invested we become in defending the uprightness of our rationalized actions. Over time, we come to sincerely believe that right is on our side, even after we have long abandoned any objective definition of ethical conduct.

Unimpeachable Logic?

A poor Jew finds a wallet with $700 in it. At his synagogue, he reads on the notice board that a wealthy congregant has lost his wallet and is offering a $100 reward for it. He spots the owner and gives him the wallet.

The rich man counts the money and says, "I see you already took your reward."

The poor man answers, "I don't understand."

"This wallet had $800 in it when I lost it. Now it's a hundred short."

They begin arguing, and eventually come before the rabbi.

Both congregants state their case. The rich man concludes by saying, "Rabbi, I trust you believe *me*."

The rabbi answers, "Of course." The rich man smiles. The poor man is crushed.

Then the rabbi hands the wallet to the poor man.

"What are you doing?!" cries the rich man.

The rabbi answers, "You are, of course, an honest man, and you say the wallet you lost had $800 in it. Therefore, I'm sure it did. But if the man who found this wallet is a liar and a thief, he wouldn't have returned it at all. That means he also is telling the truth. In that case, this wallet must belong to somebody else. If that man steps forward, he'll get the money. Until then, it belongs to the man who found it."

"But what about my money?" the rich man asks.

"Well, we'll just have to wait until somebody finds a wallet with $800 in it …"

Grapple with the Gray

    List two or three reasons to support the rich man's claim.
    List two or three reasons to support the rabbi's decision.
    Is there another option?
    Having weighed the options, did the rabbi make the right call?

Gray Matters

This little vignette is both amusing and instructive. Certainly, the rich man has reason for suspicion. Assuming that the wallet is his, someone must have taken the missing hundred. If it were anyone other than the poor man who found it, why would that person have left $700? Perhaps the poor man was simply desperate. An extra hundred dollars would be a fortune to him, and he didn't want to consider himself a thief by keeping the full $800.

On the other hand, the rich man should be delighted to recover the lion's share of the missing money. He might legitimately ask the finder if indeed he had already taken the promised reward, but once the poor man asserted he had not, the rich man should have acquiesced and been grateful to have lost $200 rather than $800. Even if he still suspected the poor man, he might consider the extra hundred a gift of charity.

With respect to the poor man, the rabbi's reasoning is based on a principle of Jewish law. In the absence of conclusive evidence, a judge must weigh the relative merit of each claim. In terms of human psychology, a person is believed that his claim is not a lie if he had a better lie available to him. If, as the rabbi explained, the poor man was a thief, he would have kept the entire $800 and never said a word. Therefore, his claim that the wallet contained only $700 is credible.

There is, however, a different angle on the matter. The sages also teach that one who admits partial guilt is suspected of being completely guilty, since an average person lacks the gall to tell a brazen lie to the face of his victim. This is borne out by modern research. Behavioral economist Dan Ariely of MIT explains that most of us don't mind stealing or cheating, as long as we can rationalize our dishonesty so that we don't have to think of ourselves as cheaters or thieves.[2]

This leaves us with competing and contradictory aspects of human nature a judge would have to consider. It also requires the judge to evaluate the prevailing sensitivities of society while determining the likelihood of a fraudulent claim.

---

[2] D. Ariely, *Predictably Irrational*, 2008. HarperCollins, New York, NY.

In an actual Jewish court, it's unlikely that a judge would rule like the rabbi in the story. The poor man admits that the money is not his, and the rich man has a legitimate claim. However, the rabbi in the story teaches a valuable lesson. Society functions best when we presume positive intent, when we give others the benefit of the doubt, and when we are grateful for small favors and partial victories that may not give us everything we want—or even everything we deserve—but still give us more than we might reasonably have expected.

Boxing for Dollars

True story:

Only after Sonny arrived at the grocery store did he remember that this was a "green" store that charged extra to supply shopping bags, and he had neglected to bring his own bags. Not wanting to pay for more bags, he stepped outside and helped himself to one of the many cardboard containers that were stacked up outside for recycling. He put the carton in his shopping cart and filled it with his groceries as he shopped.

On his way out of the store, Sonny found himself blinded by the flash of camera lights and face-to-face with a microphone.

"Congratulations!" a man said in a booming voice. "You've been chosen as the Pepsi customer of the day."

Upon further investigation, Sonny discovered that this camera crew prowls the city daily to bestow prizes on random Pepsi customers as they emerge from their shopping adventures.

"That's great," said Sonny. "But I didn't buy any Pepsi products."

"Of course you did," replied the man with the microphone. "You have a Pepsi carton right there in your shopping cart."

Only then did Sonny realize that the container he had grabbed from the front of the store was emblazoned with the Pepsi logo. Sonny immediately began explaining the mistake, but neither microphone man nor his crew seemed the least bit interested. They put a Pepsi baseball cap on Sonny's head, handed him a $100 gift card, and vanished as quickly as they had appeared.[3]

Grapple with the Gray

List two or three reasons why Sonny should return the gifts to Pepsi Co.
List two or three reasons why Sonny should keep the gifts.
Is there another alternative?
Having weighed the options as a marketer, what would you do?

---

[3]Adapted from Y. Zilberstein. 2013. *Veha'arev Na* (Jerusalem, Israel: Philipp Feldheim).

Gray Matters

Sonny certainly committed no fraud or deception. The error was entirely that of the man with the microphone, who leapt to his own conclusions and refused to listen to Sonny's protests. Nevertheless, it is generally proper to correct another's error in your favor, as when receiving too much change or discovering a miscalculation on your receipt.

However, this case seems different.

What is the purpose behind this marketing campaign? To generate excitement for a product by handing out random prizes to purchasers and publicizing the gifts to stimulate sales.

Consequently, neither Pepsi nor its potential customers know or care whether Sonny actually purchased any Pepsi products. The optics indicate that he did, and the optics are all the company cares about.

In other words, the company got exactly what it wanted, and Sonny is in no way obligated to devote his time and energy to correct a mistake that will never be noticed and in no way causes a loss to the company.

There are times when it truly seems that Providence has smiled upon us by delivering unexpected good fortune into our hands. However, we should always be on guard to ensure that our good fortune is not coming unjustly at the expense of others. Once we have determined it is not, then we can enjoy the gift from heaven with a clear conscience.

In the Bag

Are you environmentally conscientious? Have you dutifully purchased your "bags for life," those reusable shopping bags that make disposable bags unnecessary and thereby minimize your carbon footprint?

Does that make you feel good about yourself? Well, maybe it shouldn't.

Before 2019 was over, the top 10 grocery stores in Britain reported selling 1.5 billion "bags for life" since the year began, an average of 54 per household in the UK. Presumably, a typical family could get by easily with less than half-a-dozen bags and, by doing so, dramatically reduce the amount of plastic that eventually ends up in landfills.

But it doesn't seem to be working that way. Supermarkets in Britain distributed nearly 20,000 *more* tons of plastic in 2018 than they did the year before. The intended solution is merely compounding the problem.

To make matters worse, much of our home recycling practices are more placebo than cure. Families that fail to sort their trash properly end up contaminating genuine recyclables, jacking up labor and machinery repair costs. For years, much of our recycling was shipped to China for disposal. And even under ideal conditions, the cost of recycling has often made it financially impractical.

Grapple with the Gray

List two or three reasons why we should continue recycling even if it's ineffective.

List two or three reasons why we would be better off to stop ineffective recycling.

Is there another alternative?

Having weighed the options, how would you suggest addressing the global waste crisis?

Gray Matters

Our brains are lazy.

That's why we repeat the same behaviors over and over, even when we know they aren't productive, and even when we know they're counterproductive. We take comfort in familiarity, which makes us feel better by convincing us that we have the business of life well in hand.

Is that a bad thing? Sometimes, yes; sometimes, no.

Medically speaking, there are conditions where our bodies have the natural ability to fight off disease. In such cases, a placebo may boost the body's defense or healing system by promoting the confidence that comes from taking positive action.

In other cases, however, the placebo offers nothing but an illusion of intervention that may convince us that we've done enough so that we ignore the essential treatment we need to save us.

So which is it here?

Does the illusion of environmental responsibility encourage complacency, so that we exempt ourselves from implementing practices that might address our problems in a meaningful way? Or does our commitment to environmentally friendly policies keep us sensitive to the urgency of the problem, thereby increasing the likelihood that we will support beneficial policies and take more responsibility for our own actions? Will an otherwise ineffective public awareness campaign help change consumer behavior and so help progressive policies eventually succeed?

That's a question for the experts and researchers. If, over time, the sale of both "bags for life" and disposable shopping bags decline, then short-term failure may produce long-term success. How long do we have to wait? That is also a question for the experts, since human behavior often changes very slowly.

Can consumers be educated to shift their buying and disposal habits? Will recycling technology improve to become more agile and efficient?

Opinions have integrity only when they rest on a foundation of facts. Predictions have integrity only when they are based on objectively collected and evaluated data, which requires a willingness to examine both sides of an issue honestly, to encourage debate among representatives of differing perspectives, and to make mid-course corrections as new evidence shows support for one side or the other.

In the meantime, we need to continue investigating different options rather than putting all our eggs in one bag.

Unsafe at Any Speed (Part 1)

In the 1964 movie classic, *Failsafe*, American bombers are accidentally dispatched to drop nuclear bombs on Moscow. (If you haven't seen the film—*spoiler alert!*)

When the bombers cannot be recalled, the president of the United States provides the Russians with information to shoot down the planes. But one of them gets through. To prevent a massive Russian counterattack, the president orders an American bomber to drop a nuclear bomb on New York City at the same time the rogue bomb detonates over Moscow.

Grapple with the Gray
    List two or three reasons why the president made the right decision.
    List two or three reasons why the president made the wrong decision.
    Was there another alternative?
    Having weighed the options, what would you do if you were president?

Gray Matters

Some scenarios are too horrific to contemplate, which doesn't prevent us from pondering the unthinkable. Do you sacrifice millions of innocents who would later die anyway to save hundreds of millions more? The simple arithmetic favors the president's choice. But does that make it ethical?

What if an invading army demands that a city send out 10 citizens to be executed or it will kill everyone in the city? Should the citizens vote which 10 to send out? Should they choose their sacrificial lambs by lot, or ask for volunteers and hope to get some?

Even by the logic that a few lives must be forfeited to save the many, the many do not have the right to sacrifice the few. If 10 individuals want to volunteer, they may give up their lives to save others—even according to a philosophy that forbids suicide—since through no action at all they are already condemned to die. Similarly, it would be acceptable if the citizens agree unanimously on a lottery to choose the victims.

However, for a majority of citizens to hand over 10 individuals who neither volunteered nor agreed to some form of random selection would be murder, notwithstanding the inevitable murder of those same individuals by the surrounding army. No one has the right to take a life, even to save others.

For the president to order the murder of innocents, therefore, even to save the entire planet, would be immoral. The most he would be allowed to do—*perhaps*—would be to allow the Russians to bomb a major U.S. city without interference. The difference between passive and active taking of life will figure in the next scenario as well.

Unsafe at Any Speed (Part 2)

In 1967, English philosopher Philippa Foot presented what has become known as the *Trolley Problem*, in which a runaway trolley car is on course to kill five people. You are unable to warn them, but you are able to pull a switch to divert the trolley onto another track where only one person will be killed. What should you do?

Grapple with the Gray
    List two or three reasons for switching the track.
    List two or three reasons for not switching the track.
    Is there another alternative?
    Having weighed the options, what would you do?

Gray Matters

The difference between this and the *Failsafe* scenario is that your intention in diverting the trolley is to save five lives, with the single death being incidental. In contrast, the President intends to kill the people of New York and, by doing so, save many more.

Nevertheless, despite the difference in intent, you would still be actively killing one to save five.

One problem with favoring many over one is how to apply the utilitarian approach to the relative value of individuals based on their contribution to society. What if the single person is a brilliant surgeon or gifted artist who influences countless lives for the better? What if the single person is a child and the group of five are elderly? Why stop at numbers and not evaluate other factors as well?

Although few of us will ever find ourselves with such a soul-wrenching decision to make, our abstract ethical question has begun to have practical applications in the realm of artificial intelligence, most notably concerning the morality of self-driving cars.

How should computer engineers program self-driving cars to choose between fatal options, assuming the possibility of an unexpected road hazard that requires a car to take evasive action, where stopping is not a possibility? The onboard computer may have to choose between staying on course to kill five or swerving to kill only one. Perhaps a third option would be to swerve into a solid object and possibly kill the passenger or passengers.

How should the engineers program the car? Is placing the decision in the hands of AI reason enough to ban self-driving cars altogether?

Considering the number of driver-related accidents, statistical evidence suggests that self-driving cars might *reduce* the number of roadway injuries and deaths. However, for the inevitable accident, there is something in our moral programming that recoils against the idea of programming decisions that will result in a machine "deciding" to take a human life.

We can live with the idea that human error occasionally leads to injury and death. We take a certain solace from knowing that the hand of Providence guides such events and not the hand of Man. Despite the logic of the utilitarian approach, we are left with a bad taste in our mouths from the emotional unease of telling a computer which lives it should take and which lives it should spare.

***

I've long been fascinated and perplexed by the true story of a teenage girl and her mother imprisoned in a Nazi concentration camp. The daughter returned from an unusually arduous work detail to find that her mother had saved her own meager portion of soup, insisting that the daughter needed it after her day's labor. Mother and daughter each repeatedly insisted that the other needed the soup more.

Finally, the mother declared, "I'd rather pour out this soup than deprive you of it." When the daughter remained adamant, the mother poured the contents of the soup onto the ground.

At first, I found this story deeply unsettling. Why not share the soup, or choose lots? What good does it do anyone to waste the precious soup under such dire conditions?

Eventually, I came to understand. The Nazis had taken everything away from them—their homes, their families, their health, their dignity. But there was one thing that the Nazis could not take from them—their humanity. That was theirs until such time as they gave it away themselves. However impractical it was to waste the soup, the preservation of their humanity was even more important.

Practically speaking, the only choice that makes sense is to program the car to sacrifice the few for the many. But how much of our humanity will we lose by giving to a machine the power and authority to make life-and-death decisions for us?

Snake Eyes

You are the commanding officer of a military unit on patrol. One evening, after making camp in the jungle, you hear a scream. A venomous snake has crawled out of the undergrowth and wrapped itself around the leg of one of your soldiers. The soldier is terrified, and the others are afraid that any intervention will anger the snake and provoke it to bite.

You tell the soldier to stay calm and call for the unit's sniper. You instruct the soldier to remain perfectly still while the sniper shoots the snake dead.

Immediately, the soldier becomes even more agitated. He and the sniper have a history between them, having argued with each other over matters large and small from the moment they landed in the same unit. "If you let him shoot at the snake," insists the soldier, "he'll miss on purpose and hit me. Make a call to the nearest unit and have them send over their sniper."

The soldier has a point, and it should be his choice. However, you are responsible for the safety of all your men, and it will take time for another sniper to come, by which point it might be too late.

What do you do?[4]

Grapple with the Gray

List two or three reasons for using your own sniper.
List two or three reasons for calling another sniper.
Is there another alternative?
Having weighed the options, what would you do if you were the commanding officer?

---

[4]Adapted from Y. Zilberstein and M. Sherrow. 2012. *What If …* (Brooklyn, NY: Mesorah Publications).

Gray Matters

If you needed to undergo serious surgery, would you want the surgeon next door who repeatedly complained about your barking dog and your teenager's stereo? He may not want you dead, but are you eager to go under his knife? What if you were still fighting over an unresolved bill for previous medical service?

You don't really expect that the doctor will intentionally kill you. Rather, it's best practice to avoid situations where unexpected complications, emergency decisions, and hairsbreadth handiwork might conceivably be affected by attitudes and emotions. All things being equal, a different doctor would be preferable.

But what if you needed emergency surgery *right now* and your neighbor was the only surgeon available? Wouldn't that make a difference?

There's another factor also at play—professional pride.

Experts want to be recognized as experts, especially among their peers. For the sniper to miss the snake and hit his fellow soldier would cost him the respect and trust of his comrades. Whatever the sniper's feelings toward this particular soldier, self-interest would compel him to make extra-certain that his shot did not go astray.

It seems clear, therefore, that using the unit sniper irrespective of personal history is the correct choice, and ultimately in the hapless soldier's best interest—even if the soldier himself might think otherwise.

Among the many challenges of leadership is determining when to empower underlings by allowing them to make their own decisions and when to assert authority even when it seems as if the decision should belong to the individual directly involved. At the same time, leaders have to navigate the uncertain waters between wanting to be liked and needing to be respected.

The more successfully a leader responsibly asserts leadership over time, the more he or she will be trusted to do so in the future.

Gold diggers

A man bought a cemetery plot in his community cemetery. When the man passed away years later, the cemetery workers began digging his grave and, in the process, uncovered a bag of gold coins that had clearly been buried there decades earlier.

Who is entitled to the money: the cemetery owners, the gravediggers, or the heirs of the man who died?

Grapple with the Gray
    List two or three reasons why the cemetery should keep the money.
    List two or three reasons why the gravediggers should keep the money.
    List two or three reasons why the heirs should get the money.
    Is there another alternative?
    Having weighed the options, how would you resolve the question?

Gray Matters

From a purely legal point of view, the question depends on the terms of the contract. Does the future occupant of the grave site buy actual land or merely rights to use land that remains in the possession of the cemetery?

From an ethical point of view, the question is more nuanced.

The gold was on the cemetery's land. Its discovery is no different from finding a gold quarry or natural gas deposit. It belongs to the owner of the land. However, cemeteries are often owned by communities, not individuals or shareholders, in which case the discovered funds should be used for the benefit of the community.

The gravediggers were simply discharging duties for which they were getting paid. In the same way that office workers have no claim on the intellectual property they are hired and paid to produce, the gravediggers have no claim to the gold.

The question then comes to the heirs. Had their father chosen a different plot of land, the gold might have remained hidden beneath the earth until all the parties involved in the story had retired or passed on.

For the preservation of a social harmony, unexpected good fortune should not be hoarded by one party but rather shared among all who had a hand in its appearance. We might consider the case of two friends who agreed to buy a lottery ticket together. Fred paid for the ticket, and George never got around to paying for his share. When the ticket became a winner, Fred questioned whether he was obligated to share his winnings with George, who had not invested in the ticket.

Although Fred might be able to advance a strictly legal claim that the ticket was all his, it would be a pretty unsavory thing to do. He would likely destroy his relationship with George in the process. Ultimately, peace among friends and neighbors overrides all but the most clear-cut questions of money.

In this case, therefore, what seems most equitable is that the lion's share of the money remains with the cemetery and under the direction of the cemetery's board of directors to be used for communal expenses or improvement, and that a finder's fee be given to both the heirs and the gravediggers.

Leap of Faith?

About 20 years ago I was applying for life insurance. The first question on the application form asked, "Have you ever gone skydiving?"

Well, I *had* gone skydiving, but that was back when I was a reckless sophomore in college. I had no intention of ever jumping out of a plane again.

So what should I do? Should I tell the truth and risk damaging my eligibility or incurring higher premiums? Or should I lie to give a more accurate impression of who I am now?

Grapple with the Gray
- List two or three reasons why I should tell the truth on my application form.
- List two or three reasons why it's okay to lie on my application form.
- Was there another alternative?
- Having weighed the options, what would you do?

Gray Matters

In the end, I found another company. Their form asked, "Have you been skydiving in the last 10 years?" A much fairer question, to my mind.

But I still have my doubts about how I should have answered the original question.

To be sure, I understand the insurance company's intent. Why should we risk our money on the kind of people who launch themselves out of airplanes at 10,000 feet for fun? Who knows what other kinds of reckless behavior these people indulge in, and why should our other customers have to pay higher premiums to compensate for payouts to thrill-seekers and daredevils?

But personally, why should I have to pay more for a youthful indiscretion when, decades later, I have far too much common sense to take needless chances with my life for a few moments of adrenaline rush?

Perhaps the ethical question here has more to do with the phrasing of their question than with the accuracy of my answer.

What happens when we put people in situations where they have to choose between honesty and self-interest? Sometimes it may be inevitable, but what if it's not? Aren't our lives already filled with enough conflicts that challenge our internal moral code?

In this case, hadn't enough time gone by to allow me to let my past remain buried in the past? In fact, didn't the last 20 years of responsible behavior testify that I was indeed a good risk, that I had learned from past mistakes and charted a new course into the future?

A number of recent scandals demonstrate the immediacy of these questions. Public figures who, 20 years ago or more, appeared in black face or tweeted ethnic slurs are not allowed to apologize or disavow their behavior without repercussions, no matter how sincerely contrite they may appear.

We aren't talking about serious incidents of sexual abuse, pedophilia, extortion, or murder which might, legitimately, have no statute of limitations. We're talking about bad taste, immaturity, or personal biases that most of us have experienced to some degree and hopefully outgrown.

When a society refuses to acknowledge sincere repentance and recognize that the responsible citizens of today often traveled the road of irresponsibility to get where they are, we encourage and perpetuate bad behavior: Why should anyone strive to be better if we will be held prisoners of our past for the rest of our lives? Indeed, Jewish law forbids embarrassing another person by reminding him of a past he has put behind him.

Even the innocuous wording on a life insurance form promotes this kind of wrongheaded attitude. If I have to lie about mistakes I've made and corrected to be respected for who I am now, am I not trapped in a paradox that hampers my efforts to be virtuous and thereby condemns me to remain corrupt?

We serve no one when we indulge such a system.

Eye-to-I

Imagine the following scenario—it won't be difficult.

Two candidates, each vying for support to represent their party in the presidential election, have been grappling over issues for months. Inevitably, one prevails over the other and wins the nomination. As the national convention progresses, the winner taps the loser as his or her vice-presidential running mate.

The two retire for a private meeting to hash out the details. After a couple of hours, the new candidate for VP emerges before a battalion of microphones and cameras to announce his acceptance.

"But what about all the policy differences you so hotly debated throughout the primary race?" one reporter asks. "How can you join this ticket when you and the presidential nominee have such divergent positions?"

"The two of us spent a long time discussing these issues," comes the smooth reply, "and our future president has convinced me that his opinion on each of these issues is the correct one."

What are we to think of this candidate and his response?

Grapple with the Gray

List two or three reasons in defense of the candidate's reply.
List two or three reasons for being critical of the candidate's reply.
Was there another way he might have responded?
Having weighed the options, as a politician, what would you do?

Gray Matters

The most obvious problem with the candidate's reply is that no one is going to believe him. After months of speeches, debates, and interviews, it's ludicrous to think that he could be convinced to reverse his position on a wide range of core issues after a 2-hour conversation.

But let's examine the candidate's dilemma.

He wants to support his own party candidate. He believes that this candidate will make a far superior president than the candidate from the other party. He wants to influence the direction of the country from within the White House. He understands that as VP he must support the policies of his president regardless of his own personal views.

Clearly, he cannot continue to advocate for his own policies if he accepts the nomination. But does that mean he has to publicly recant them all, thereby calling into question his own honesty and integrity? By answering as he did, he leaves the public no choice but to look at him as either a liar or a jellyfish.

Now imagine that he answered as follows:

"No two people can or should agree on everything, and that includes the two names on any presidential ticket. Having a variety of opinions and points of view ensures more reasoned discussions, more thoughtful decisions, and fewer policy errors."

"However, all decisions will be the president's, and I will support those decisions because I respect this candidate's ability and integrity, and because I believe this candidate to be the person most qualified to do the job."

Wouldn't that be refreshing?

Virtual Dominoes

In 1988, archeologist Joseph Tainter published his most famous work, *The Collapse of Complex Societies*. The book issued a warning—one echoed by sociologists, futurists, and science fiction writers—that the more complex our society becomes, the more vulnerable we are.

This is now painfully obvious from the countless incidents of identity theft, the growing threat of cyberterrorism, and the relatively new scourge of ransomware. Often unreported by institutional victims around the world who worry as much about their brand integrity as their bottom line, online criminals implant viruses that freeze users out of their own systems, then demand extortion money to return users access to their own computers.

Aside from businesses and corporations, victims include hospitals, whose patients' lives are endangered by crippled emergency and diagnostic equipment.

This raises all kinds of ethical questions. Should the National Security Agency be held responsible, since the original virus was stolen from them? Should Microsoft be allowed to charge a hefty fee for fixing software that cash-strapped hospitals couldn't afford to have protected? Should victims pay extortion money to restore their own systems to functionality when, by doing so, they encourage cyber-extortionists to target more victims?

Grapple with the Gray

List two or three reasons why victims should pay the ransom.

List two or three reasons why no ransom should be paid.

List two or three reasons why NSA or Microsoft should be held responsible.

Having weighed the options, what do you think should be done?

Gray Matters

Many of the ethical questions raised here have already appeared in less dramatic form. If an insured motorist gets hit by an uninsured motorist, does the insurance company have the right to raise the insured motorist's rates? Is it fair that hospitals give care to uninsured patients, passing those costs along to paying patients or their insurance companies? Surely it can't be right to withhold patient care because of inability to pay, can it?

What would you say about the case of firemen watching a house burn down because the owner refused to pay voluntary taxes to support the fire department? If homeowners know that the fire department will protect their homes even if they don't pay, won't they be more likely to withhold payment? And if homeowners refuse to pay for the fire department until they need it, then the fire department can't afford to operate in the first place.

Ethical questions like these don't always have clear answers. What if two people are drowning and there's only one life vest?

The real answer is to provide enough life vests before the ship sinks.

We can never protect against everything. But if we don't plan for reasonable contingencies, then we bring trouble down on our own heads. It might be unethical for others to deny us help when we need it, but exposing ourselves to unnecessary risk and counting on others to come to our rescue—that's unethical itself.

So let's work backwards. The question of ransom has been debated for centuries. Long ago, it was pirates who held captives for ransom. If no ransom is paid, pirates will stop taking hostages. But how can we condemn an innocent hostage to death or captivity now to spare some future, hypothetical hostage?

In 1801, the newly elected President Thomas Jefferson sent the U.S. marines into Tripoli to put an end to state-sponsored piracy along the Barbary Coast. Treaties, tributes, and an international policing coalition had all failed to curb North African pirates, and Mr. Jefferson turned to the final resort.

In many ways, the decision to intervene was a financial one. It was less expensive, in the long run, to pay for an invasion force than to leave American shipping at continual risk.

Sometimes, we need financial pressure to get us to do the right thing. But leaving ethical decisions in the hands of market forces is a poor formula for building an ethical society. Just the opposite is true: an ethical culture will allow free markets to flourish free from corruption.

If the NSA set the virus loose on the public, it is no less responsible than a landowner or camper whose bonfire burns out of control and starts a forest fire. If Microsoft has the ability to restore vital services to a hospital, it has an ethical responsibility to discount its rates to ensure the well-being of patients.

The common denominator, however, is foresight. Indeed, when the sage Rabbi Shimon was asked to identify the straight path one should walk in life, he replied: "To anticipate every outcome."

Each member of a society shares responsibility to contribute evenly to preserve the necessary services that allow a society to function. But evenly is not always the same as equally. Accommodations must be made for those in more difficult circumstances. Still, no one should be let completely off the hook. Only when every citizen is an investor can society as a whole reap the profits of prosperity.

On Thin Ice

In December 2019, a Russian figure skater appeared on the ice to the theme from *Schindler's List*, Steven Spielberg's cinematic masterpiece about the Holocaust. The skater's choice of music might have passed without comment if not for his choice of costume: a striped shirt in the style of a Nazi concentration camp uniform emblazoned with a large, yellow star-of-David.

To complicate matters, the International Skating Union proceeded to nominate the skater for the best costume award of the competition. After the predictable outcry, the ISU responded with a predictable apology, claiming that the judges had meant to nominate the skater for the costume he had worn in his *other* program.

Contributing to the hasty apology was, presumably, condemnation by the Anti-Defamation League of both the costume and the ISU. CEO Jonathan A. Greenblatt issued this statement:

"While we understand the need for skaters to be creative in their choice of costumes, [the skater's] apparent decision to evoke painful Holocaust imagery as part of his routine was insensitive and offensive.

We are surprised that the International Skating Union initially posted a picture of this costume as a nominee for 'costume of the year.' Yellow Stars of David or other concentration camp imagery have no place in figure skating."

Grapple with the Gray

- List two or three reasons in defense of the skater and his costume choice.
- List two or three reasons why the skater was wrong in his choice of costume.
- Could the skater have devised a different costume to fit the music?
- After thoughtful consideration, what would you have done if you were the skater, or a member of the ISU?

Gray Matters

There is a tendency to overreact to these kinds of stories, which is why Jonathan Greenblatt's measured response was reassuring. He recognized the offensive costume choice as a lapse of sensitivity rather than an act of malice, while acknowledging that creativity—by definition—tends to challenge accepted norms.

If anything, Mr. Greenblatt may have gone too far in the restraint he showed addressing the ISU, which has far less excuse for being culturally tone-deaf than a 23-year-old Eastern European skater.

We learn the basic principles of social skills from our parents, teachers, and peers. Then, we need to fine-tune those skills largely through trial and error. That's why 20-year-old Prince Harry recovered his reputation after showing up at a costume party in 2005 sporting the uniform of a Nazi officer. Despite the faux pas, the young royal seems to have grown up nicely into a respectable and respectful adult.

The boundaries between avant-garde and bad taste are fluid and often difficult to define. In a context evoking sorrow, hopelessness, oppression, or evil, an Auschwitz-style uniform might be entirely appropriate. In the festive context of a skating tournament, it shows disrespect for the suffering of millions at the hands of history's most notorious criminals.

The confusion among many young people—and too many adults—to discern where those boundaries lie is compounded by the recent, first-world phenomenon of "cultural appropriation." In a bizarre ideological paradox, the same progressive voices that have fought to erase the boundaries between males and females have simultaneously determined that ethnic traditions are sacrosanct and are forbidden to any but their rightful inheritors.

As a result, Caucasian school children have been censured for wearing Asian attire. Safari-themed resorts have been boycotted for violating African cultural integrity. Sports teams have changed their names to avoid offending Native Americans, and a popular Volkswagen television ad was condemned for portraying a white office employee who spoke with a Jamaican accent.

I asked a Jamaican friend what he thought of the ad; he loved it. Personally, anyone who wants to dress up as a chassidic Jew on Halloween may do so with my blessing. And what harm the Kalahari Resorts are doing to people in Africa or of African descent is beyond me.

Somewhere in the middle is the controversy over sports teams branded with Native American names. The argument that these names were given with intent to demean or discriminate seems disingenuous. Why would any team want to be named for a group it did not admire? Rather, names like the Braves, the Chiefs, and the Redskins were chosen presumably to evoke and honor the fighting spirit associated with those indigenous peoples.

According to reports, there is some variance of opinion within the Native American community. Some find the use of their cultural images flattering and complimentary; others find that same use insulting and given to perpetuate cultural stereotypes and discrimination.

Ultimately, it is the opinion of Native Americans alone that matters. However, in a culture that increasingly seeks out malicious intent where clearly none was intended, it's incumbent upon all groups and individuals to examine their own motives.

Do Native American mascots perpetuate degrading stereotypes and contribute to real psychological pain and societal harm? If so, they should go. But if objections arise primarily from an abstract claim that cultural identity has simply been "misappropriated," it's worth examining how far any of us should have to go to protect others from the mere *perception* of offense.

Ethics depends on value judgments. And the more cloudy our values become, the more difficult it is for us to identify the boundaries of ethical behavior.

As an endnote, some might find a comforting irony to learn that the skater sporting the Holocaust costume finished in last place.

Why Vote?

Most of us have probably pondered this question at one time or another. In presidential elections, we may live in states where the results are a foregone conclusion—no matter how we vote, our vote is not going to change the outcome.

Even in smaller elections, the chances of one vote making a difference are only slightly better than getting hit by lightning or winning the lottery. Has it happened? Sure, it has. A few times. But less than once in a dozen blue moons, and never in an election with more than 25,000 voters.

Statistically speaking, it's almost certain that neither your vote nor mine is going to make any difference in the outcome of any election.

We consider voting an act of civic duty. But what is the point of a duty that has no measurable effect?

Grapple with the Gray
    List two or three reasons why every citizen should vote.
    List two or three reasons not to vote.
    Are there any other options?
    Having weighed the options, will you vote?

Gray Matters

One of my mentors, Rabbi Dovid Gottlieb, PhD, offers the following scenario:

Imagine that you live in a small town at the bottom of a deep ravine. One afternoon, a messenger arrives with news that the dam above your town is showing signs of stress and is expected to collapse in 24 hours.

The town council meets with experts, who conclude that the construction of a stone wall upstream would diffuse the floodwaters and save the town. In order to build such a wall, every one of the town's 1,000 residents will have to carry a stone block 3 miles to the designated location. With a thousand stones, the wall will be strong and high enough to save the town.

The next day, you wake up to a cold, drizzly morning. Everyone has agreed to meet in the town square shortly after sunrise to begin carrying the stones. But the last thing you want to do is go out in the cold and damp to lug a heavy rock 3 miles. So you start making mental calculations:

What if nobody else goes? Your one stone won't make any difference, and the town will be destroyed.

What if everybody else goes? Your one stone won't be missed—999 is as good as a thousand—and the town will be saved.

What if some people go—400 ... 800 ... 673; will that be enough? Maybe, maybe not. In any event, your one stone will not make a difference.

Do you roll over and go back to sleep? What you might do is look back out the window. If you see a lot of people on their way to carry their stones, you're more likely to ask yourself how you can stay comfortably in your bed when others are trekking out to save your home. Whether you feel guilt, shame, or embarrassment, there's a good chance you'll get up and go carry your stone.

But what if you see empty streets? You might ask yourself why you should go trudging toward the foot of the mountains when no one else cares enough to go. Or you might wonder instead whether your neighbors are waiting for someone else to go first and show them that their community is worth fighting to save.

This by itself should be enough reason to act or, in our case, enough reason to vote. A community survives only when its members are committed to its survival and its prosperity. After all, what is a community but a collection of individuals bound together by a common sense of identity, values, and commitment? If we don't care enough to save our community, then it really isn't worth saving.

One person's commitment strengthens another's. Especially in times when we have to choose between candidates who are uninspiring at best and loathsome at worst, it becomes essential to declare and to demonstrate that we haven't given up on our society or on the system that defines it.

That's what it means to be a member of a community and a good citizen. That's why every vote really does make a difference.

PART 5

Ethical Headlines

Those whose good deeds exceed their wisdom, their wisdom will endure; those whose wisdom exceeds their good deeds, their wisdom will not endure.

—Ethics of Fathers 3:12

All for One?

In May 2019, Delta Airlines circulated a flyer encouraging employees, instead of paying $700 on their annual union dues, to spend the money on a new video game player. Predictably, the company came under fire from employees, pundits, and presidential hopeful Bernie Sanders. With Delta's CEO earning somewhere between 13 and 22 million dollars a year (depending on your source), many described the circular in such terms as *crass, condescending, disgusting,* and *disgraceful.*

There was a time when unions truly represented the underdogs, coming to the defense of workers unable to fight back against slave wages, onerous hours, and unsafe work conditions. Over time, however, unions grew into powers of their own, investing their large war chests not only in the cause of employee protection and advocacy, but increasingly into political activism.

Many dues-paying union members have come to resent how their money gets spent. But they've found themselves as helpless to influence union political activity as their great-grandfathers were to influence unethical employer practices. Some of them would like to withdraw from union membership altogether.

The unions have argued that they support candidates and causes that favor workers. They also argue that through their negotiations, all employees enjoy the advantages of higher wages and more comprehensive benefits. Therefore, it wouldn't be equitable for some employees to bear the expense of supporting the union when all employees reaped the rewards of union efforts on employees' behalf.

Grapple with the Gray
   List two or three reasons for mandatory union membership.
   List two or three reasons for optional union membership.
   Is there another option?
   Having weighed the options, what do you say about union membership and policy?

Gray Matters

Four months after the controversial flyer appeared—on Labor Day, in fact—Delta announced a 4 percent pay raise for its non-union employees. The following January, it gave every employee a profit-sharing bonus of 2 months' salary. Only company officers, directors and general managers were excluded.

In contrast to unionized American Airlines, Delta seemed to be flying high.

Despite the brouhaha over the offending circular, Delta has been long admired for the quality of its company culture, where employees feel fairly treated, recognized for their efforts, and part of a purpose-driven team. Studies have shown that many members of the larger workforce value the quality of their work environment more than money.

The very concept of unions implies contention between management and employees. Too often, employees need unions to protect their interests against self-serving owners and combative management. But when bosses and managers demonstrate a willingness to meet employees half-way, to listen to their needs and concerns, to respond to their suggestions and grievances, then employees feel empowered and appreciated, obviating the need for a union at all.

Of course, you have healthy and unhealthy company cultures, so it's impractical to make a blanket rule for whether unions are truly justified and—when they are—whether employees should have freedom to withdraw. Clearly, there is something inequitable about employees benefiting from union negotiations on their behalf when they don't pay union dues.

Even when unions are necessary, the next question becomes how to measure and monitor when they cross the line from advocacy to activism. Simply putting policy decisions to a vote is not entirely equitable. An employee might reasonably argue as follows: When the union donates money to a candidate I don't like, I'm paying more for my benefits than I should be, as well as paying for activities I don't recognize as beneficial.

The beginnings of a solution might be to give employees the option whether their dues money may be used to support political candidates, causes, and committees, thereby capping the amount of money available for political donations. Members might be able to declare party affiliation, with donations being divided among parties and candidates proportionately.

In a perfect world, management would make employee welfare so intricately aligned with company culture that unions would become unnecessary. Until that happens, unions will remain an essential, if imperfect, part of the business landscape.

In or Out?

In July 2017, a mere 2 months before the fall semester was set to begin, the University of California at Irvine rescinded the admissions of 499 students it had previously accepted.

The administration originally claimed that these incoming students had failed to meet the deadline for submitting their official transcripts, although never before had the university disinvited students for that reason.

Eventually, the school admitted it had overbooked its freshman class, underestimating the number of students who would confirm their enrollment.

One student had turned down a $30,000 scholarship to another school to attend UCI, which he couldn't get back. Another had a 4.11 high school GPA. Many were left with no good options.

Was the university wrong?

Grapple with the Gray
- List two or three reasons in defense of the university's decision.
- List two or three reasons why the university was wrong.
- Were there any other options?
- Having weighed the options, what would you have done if you were an admissions officer?

Gray Matters

UCI's rejection of previously accepted students is little better than United Airlines dragging Dr. David Dao off their plane because they had overbooked the flight and needed his seat. As a rule, even the airlines understand that overbooking is the airline's problem to fix at its own expense, not at the passengers'. In any contractual agreement, you're obliged to pay full compensation when you renege on a commitment.

This is why colleges have something called a *waiting list*, so prospective students know where they stand. Students do not deserve to have their college careers derailed by administrators who don't know how to fix their own mistakes.

It's true that by missing the transcript submission deadline the students set themselves up for potential consequences. But the reaction needs to be proportionate to the offense. In this case, the university handed down a felony sentence in response to a misdemeanor crime merely as a smokescreen to conceal its own faux pas, exploiting the letter of the law to pervert the spirit of the law.

As we've already discussed, that is precisely what ethics is—or is not—about.

This is what happens when the moral compass of a culture stops pointing forward. If we want to benefit from living in a civil society and not revert to the law of the jungle, we can't afford to ignore our responsibilities to others and the effect our actions have on those around us, even if we can quote legal chapter and verse to defend our actions.

It's not a stretch to argue that this same mindset has contributed to incidents of sexual harassment at Uber and Fox News, phony accounts created at Wells Fargo, and the collusion revealed by the Panama Papers, with the proliferation of scandals seeming to increase every year.

The more corrupt people in power become, the more corruption becomes accepted and acceptable. The less we recognize moral corruption for what it is, the more likely we are to rationalize it in our own lives.

In the end, UCI readmitted most of the students. But the decision seemed a response to public disapproval rather than an expression of genuine contrition. Before you get caught trying to cut ethical corners, consider what's right rather than what's convenient. Be true to your word, so that others will trust you. In return, they will want to earn your trust. When we live in a society governed by ethics, all of us come out ahead.

Crying Wolf?

In February 2017, Dr. John Bates made headlines by claiming that his former boss, Thomas Karl of the National Oceanic and Atmospheric Administration, had knowingly misrepresented data to influence government policy on global warming.

Predictably, climate change skeptics railed against the corruption of the scientific community, while climate change advocates charged Dr. Bates with exaggerating his claims.

For the sake of argument, let's assume that the charges are true. If so, it's likely that Dr. Karl was motivated by the purest intentions, that he wanted to spur action to prevent what he genuinely believed to be the devastating effects of global warming, and that he viewed the data as representing an anomaly rather than a larger global trend.

If all of that were actually true, would he have then been justified in doctoring the facts for the greater good?

Grapple with the Gray
- List two or three reasons in defense of Dr. Karl.
- List two or three reasons why Dr. Karl would have been wrong to misrepresent the data.
- Was there another alternative?
- Having weighed the options, as a scientist, what would you do?

Gray Matters

Writing in Forbes Magazine, Michael Shellenberger, founder and president of Environmental Progress, argued that misreporting on climate science carries unintended consequences. He cited a British study that found anxiety levels among children rising considerably faster than sea levels and blamed overzealous environmental activists for provoking violence in the streets.

What's more, inaccurate reporting undermines support for the cause itself. "There is good evidence that the catastrophist framing of climate change is self-defeating," Mr. Shellenberger writes, "because it alienates and polarizes many people."

More than that, the doomsayers discredit their own science and their own position. Way back when Al Gore began sounding the drum for climate change, he foretold that if the advance of global warming was not halted by 2010, it would be too late to save the planet. Was he wrong then, or is he wrong a decade after the deadline as he continues to advocate for climate reform?

True, sensationalist claims make for great headlines and attention-grabbing sound bites. Once exposed, however, they provide ammunition to the other side, enabling opponents to legitimately discount *all* reported data based on the demonstrable indictment that environmental activists are untrustworthy.

The same principle applies in any debate. Whether it's climate, the economy, abortion, supreme court nominations, impeachment investigations, universal health care, or tax policy, the flow of misinformation and exaggerated rhetoric from both sides makes it nearly impossible for even the most clear-thinking voters to resolve contradictions by filtering out hyperbole and genuinely fake news.

In the end, everyone suffers. Either we lose hope of achieving clarity or we take refuge in the opinions of whichever "experts" tell us what we want to hear.

As a consumer of news, it's critical to choose carefully the outlets where you get your information, and to expose yourself to responsible sources and commentators representing both sides of the debate. If you listen to only one side on any issue, you set yourself up to make unethical decisions—particularly if that side disseminates skewed facts and slanted commentary.

Even well-intentioned reporters face the challenge of striking the right balance when presenting complex topics for popular consumption. Unfiltered data can increase confusion and create false impressions. On the other hand, it's easy to rationalize selectively presenting information that supports one's own agenda.

With one step in that direction, down the slippery slope we go, ending up in an ethical quagmire without noticing how we got there. We might be right in principle. But once the truth comes out, the damage done to our reputation and our cause may be irreparable.

Standing on Principle?

Shortly after his inauguration in January 2017, President Donald Trump fired acting Attorney General Sally Yates for refusing to defend an executive order imposing a temporary ban on refugees from countries connected with terrorist activity. Ms. Yates explained her position in a letter claiming that she was not "convinced" of the legality of the law.

Some legal authorities argued that Ms. Yates did not provide adequate justification for her refusal, failing to demonstrate *or even claim* that the order was unconstitutional. Apparently, it was her own personal bias, rather than the actual legality of the executive order, that influenced Ms. Yates to make her decision.

This episode hearkened back to September 2015, when County Clerk Kim Davis refused to issue marriage licenses for gay couples as required by newly passed marriage laws in Kentucky. Ms. Davis cited her religious beliefs as the reason for her refusal.

Not surprisingly, the same conservatives who applauded Kim Davis for her act of conscience castigated Ms. Yates for hers; and the same liberals who cheered on Ms. Yates were outraged by Ms. Davis' contempt for the law.

From an ethical, rather than a political perspective, who was right?

Grapple with the Gray

List two or three reasons why the two cases are similar.
List two or three reasons why the two cases are dissimilar.
Did the two women have another option?
Having weighed the options, what would you have done?

Gray Matters

If you had difficulty articulating a difference between the two cases, congratulations on your intellectual integrity. From a purely objective, nonpartisan viewpoint, it's hard to find a substantive argument to differentiate between them.

It's disingenuous, therefore, to either defend or condemn one of these women and not the other. Although civil disobedience and acts of conscience are both core values in American tradition, from an ethical perspective the action of either woman is difficult to justify.

An oath of office is administered because public service is an act of public trust. We are allowed to disagree with our lawmakers, even challenge them and lobby against them, as long as we do so within the boundaries of the law. If you find yourself in a situation where you cannot serve both your conscience and your duty, then your only ethical option is to resign your position.

But neither woman chose that option. Each wanted to keep her position while declaring the demands of performing it unjust. But you can't have it both ways; and attempting to do so leads to anarchy. If you want to make a statement of conscience, make it all the way or not at all. otherwise you are exploiting conscience in the service of ideology.

And that is profoundly unethical.

At times, ethical duty may indeed require us to break the law. But that same code of ethics requires us to accept the consequences of our actions, not try to hide from them behind a mask of questionable integrity.

Paved with Good Intentions

In 2002, Republican Senator John McCain and Democrat Senator Russ Feingold succeeded in passing their bipartisan finance reform bill, limiting the contributions by large donors to any political party or candidate.

In principle, the passage of the bill was a victory for electoral integrity, restoring more power to lower- and middle-class donors in support of political candidates and causes. In practice, it had just the opposite effect.

According to the Washington Post, money that had once gone to the national parties was redirected to political action committees, leaving the party leadership with less resources and less motivation to recruit and encourage grassroots participation. As it turns out, the parties previously had a moderating effect on partisanship by needing to achieve some degree of interparty consensus. Independent advocacy groups have no such compunctions.

Consequently, the effect of finance reform was to marginalize the moderates and give even more influence to big money players—exactly the opposite of what was intended.

Hindsight is 20/20, and unintended consequences are inevitable. When we see systemic problems and want to correct them, should we do our best to implement solutions knowing they might backfire, or should we leave well enough alone and make peace with the devil we know?

Grapple with the Gray
　　List two or three reasons why the finance reform law was worth trying.
　　List two or three reasons why the sponsors of the bill should have left well enough alone.
　　Were there any other options?
　　Having weighed the options, as a lawmaker how would you have made your decision?

Gray Matters

In the year 70, the Second Temple in Jerusalem was destroyed by the Roman legions after a protracted siege of the city. According to Jewish history, the spark that ignited the fury of Rome was kindled by a disgruntled Jew named Bar Kamtza who slandered his own people by accusing the sages of inciting rebellion against the occupying government.

As events unfolded, the sages learned of the danger Bar Kamtza posed and held counsel to determine how they might stop his intrigue. Although one proposal after another was put forth to prevent the approaching apocalypse, one of the sages, Rabbi Zechariah, raised an objection to each. As a result, the sages failed to take any action whatsoever. Bar Kamtza's plot succeeded, the Roman army descended, and Jerusalem was destroyed.

Rabbi Zechariah's objections were reasonable and well-founded. Nevertheless, later generations blamed him for the destruction of the Temple, even more than Bar Kamtza and more than the Romans themselves. By prolonging the debate, while failing to offer any practical alternative, Rabbi Zechariah paralyzed the high council of sages and guaranteed that all the suffering that befell the nation would follow.

In other words, there are always good reasons not to take action. But no decision is also a decision; and it's often a worse choice than a wrong decision.

Consider the Bill and Melinda Gates Global Fund, which has seen tremendous success eliminating malaria, measles, and AIDS from sub-Saharan Africa. While accomplishing its goals, the high-profile project has had the unintended consequence of drawing medical experts away from less glamorous positions, at times leaving laypeople responsible for education, triage, and low-level nursing, especially in rural areas. A lack of basic supplies not covered by the fund has resulted in avoidable tragedies.

More recently, the release of sterilized mosquitoes has some scientists worried about unpredictable environmental effects.

So was the Gates Foundation wrong to attempt eliminating disease?

Of course not. Nevertheless, these stories serve as cautionary tales against attempting to play God. The FDA has often been criticized for its overcautious approach to releasing new drugs and treatment. But that conservative approach saved countless American children in the 1950s from the side effects of thalidomide, an innovative morning sickness drug responsible for horrific birth defects in 10,000 European babies.

Like every other application of ethics, sincere and well-reasoned balance between action and caution must guide medical and legislative intervention. Unintended consequences are inevitable. The question will always be whether we have taken all reasonable precautions to avoid them, rather than rushing impetuously into action or wringing our hands over our inability to act.

Whistleblowing in the Dark?

In 2013, Eric Snowden leaked documents to the press revealing a vast program of government surveillance over American citizens. According to intelligence officials, the documents released by Snowden put U.S. personnel and facilities around the world at risk, damaged further intelligence efforts, exposed intelligence tools and operations, destabilized U.S. partnerships across the globe, hindered the prevention of terrorist activity, and endangered the lives of operatives and private citizens.

Some see Snowden as a traitor; others see him as a hero. Former U.S. Attorney General Eric Holder straddled the fence, praising Snowden for performing a "public service" by sparking debate over surveillance techniques, but asserting that he must still pay a penalty for leaking classified intelligence documents.

The potential for whistleblowing provides an essential check on both corporate and government abuses of power and disregard for the law. Often, whistleblowers are indeed heroes, risking their liberty, their livelihoods, and sometimes their lives to expose criminality. There's good reason why whistleblowers should be protected with anonymity, lest fear of retaliation frighten them into silence and allow corruption to increase unchecked.

But what about the rights of the accused to confront their accusers, which was withheld in the impeachment investigation of President Donald Trump? How do we balance providing safety for whistleblowers with ensuring justice for the accused? And how do we determine when the collateral damage of whistleblowers' evidence outweighs the benefits of their information?

Grapple with the Gray

- List two or three reasons why Eric Snowden should be considered a hero.
- List two or three reasons why Snowden should be considered a traitor. Did he have any other options?
- Having weighed the options, what would you do if you discovered corruption but knew that innocent people might be hurt through its revelation?

Gray Matters

Professor Stephen L. Carter asserts that integrity requires us not only to do the right thing but to take full responsibility for our decisions by facing the consequences of doing what's right. From the point of ideological purity, that is absolutely true. But what if the consequences seem disproportionate to the decision? And what if others who had no say in my decision will suffer on my account?

Consider the corporate whistleblower who exposes scandalous conduct and, by doing so, loses his job. What if he finds himself threatened with crushing legal expenses to defend himself from violating his nondisclosure agreement and possible jail time? Will we think less of him for declining to act with integrity in order to protect himself and his family?

On the other hand, without consequences we have far less assurance of the credibility of whistleblowers, who may themselves be looking for revenge after being passed over for a promotion or losing their jobs due to poor performance. The willingness to put themselves at risk is part of what makes whistleblowers' testimony so compelling.

There's also the abstract value of personal privacy weighed against the very real consequences of action or inaction. Does my right to speak privately to my wife on my cell phone trump the right of thousands to be protected from potential terrorism by way of government surveillance? What about the right to have a provocative conversation with my mistress, to plan embezzling from my employer or cheat on my taxes? When do the benefits of government surveillance override the potential abuse of power that government officials might be subject to as imperfect human beings?

There are no simple answers to these questions. But returning to Professor Carter's observation, the willingness to risk the consequences of integrity may be the most compelling way to contribute to a culture of integrity, one in which whistleblowers feel that they will at least be treated fairly and that their sacrifices will make a difference.

Imagine how ethical our society would be if we had more examples like Pastor Martin Niemöller, imprisoned from 1937 to 1945 in the Sachsenhausen and Dachau concentration camps for speaking out against the rise of Nazism in prewar Germany. He didn't slow the horrors perpetrated by the Nazis with his sacrifice. But he did survive the war, passing away in his nineties and outliving his persecutors by four decades. He leaves behind his heroic commitment to truth, and his poetic indictment of all those who looked the other way and allowed evil to flourish:

> First, they came for the Communists, and I didn't speak out because I wasn't a Communist.
>
> Then they came for the trade unionists, and I didn't speak out because I wasn't a trade unionist.
>
> Then they came for the Jews, and I didn't speak out because I wasn't a Jew.
>
> Then they came for me, and there was no one left to speak.

Afterword

Shin Dong-hyuk was born in Kaechon internment camp #14 in North Korea. He grew up with no knowledge of the outside world. He never heard of things we take for granted, like money, love, or God.

He had no loyalty to his family, only to the guards who held reward and punishment in their hands. And he had no motivation to escape, until a fellow inmate told him that there was a different world on the other side of the prison fence. Even after escaping to South Korea, he struggled to understand and absorb the values that most of us accept as moral axioms.

The Jewish sages would have labeled Shin Dong-hyuk a *tinok she'nishba*, a child kidnapped and raised in a society of thieves. Even as an adult, such a person has no culpability for his actions, since he may never successfully uproot the values of criminality he absorbed growing up and replace them with the values of right and wrong. Because of his upbringing, he may suffer from terminal moral blindness.

The truth is, we are all born into the prisons of our respective environments, which can blind us to ideas and perspectives that reside beyond the comfort zone of intellectual familiarity.

This blindness takes one of two forms. The first is where we know we can't see; at least then we can seek out others who possess vision and turn to them for guidance. Far more dangerous is where we believe that we see clearly when in fact our vision is impaired. Then we proceed with confidence, oblivious to the consequences of our blindness.

Moral vision requires us to expand our awareness of others by learning to recognize the social cues that govern human interaction. Without that awareness we cannot acquire empathy, which is critical to living a life of ethics.

The little niceties that are rapidly disappearing from society are more than arbitrary conventions. When you say *please* and *thank you*, when you use a correspondent's name in an e-mail, when you silence your phone in meetings and in your place of worship, when you don't keep others waiting unnecessarily, when you lower your voice in public, hold the elevator door, look others in the eye and smile, refrain from gossip, tuck in your chair, don't roll your stops at stop signs, and *really* listen when others are speaking—all these simple acts of respect for those around you and for the society you live in serve as constant reminders that what you do matters, that your little actions make a big difference.

Even the smallest act of thoughtful awareness keeps you attuned to the nuances of speech and behavior that are integral to an ethical mindset. Etiquette is more than a code of social graces observed by the privileged classes; etiquette is the art of social ethics.

But we need to learn the right cues from the right people. Do you remember when your parent said to you, "If Pat jumped off the roof, would you do it, too?" Do you remember saying it to your own child? (If you haven't yet, you probably will.)

There's a lot of wisdom in that parental cliché … in almost every cliché, really. Clichés become clichés because their self-evident truth makes us repeat them again and again, which is unfortunate. Any truism that becomes part of the cultural landscape is eventually no longer noticed and, subsequently, becomes forgotten.

The invisibility of the overly familiar is just one trick our subconscious minds play to trip us up. Look back through the chapters of this book and notice how you answered the last question after each case study—the "what would you do?" question. Do you find that you more frequently agreed with the position you defended first versus the opposing position you tried to defend second? If so, it's likely not a coincidence.

A decades-old psychology experiment asked subjects to compose a list of reasons for buying a video-cassette recorder, and then asked them to compose a list of reasons not to buy one. The researchers asked the same two questions to a second group, but in reverse order. In both cases, the subjects reported that they had more difficulty coming up with reasons to answer the second question after answering the first. They also reported that their answers to the first question influenced their buying decisions, both at the time of the survey and several weeks later.[1]

---

[1] D.J. Koehler. 1991. "Explanation, Imagination, and Confidence in Judgment." *Psychological Bulletin* 110, no. 3, pp. 499–519.

This demonstrates how quickly and easily we invest ourselves in any point of view, and how difficult it is to uproot attitudes and perspectives once we commit ourselves to them. It also explains why many news outlets consistently structure their reporting by leading with the information or perspective that supports their own editorial slant; they know that what audiences hear first will become more deeply implanted in their long-term memories, shaping their own attitudes and points of view.

If we want to acquire the even-handedness critical to an ethical mindset, we need to recognize the mechanistic workings of our minds and compensate for our natural and unconscious biases. Sometimes that requires us to choose which subjects we don't talk about as much as which subjects we do.

The thoughtful reader may be wondering why so many obvious topics of ethical debate remain absent from this book. Abortion, climate change, gun control, taxation, the Me Too movement, and the endless assortment of peculiar practices found among the denizens of the political zoo—any or all of these would have provided easy and valuable fodder for ethical discourse.

The sad reality is that many of us lack the intellectual detachment to evaluate hot-button issues on their own merits without plunging into ideology or character assassination. In fact, our confidence that our cause is just—regardless of which side we are on—breeds intellectual arrogance and complacency, convincing us we don't need to deeply research or reason through our own positions. This in turn leaves us haunted by the suspicion that we can't defend our causes, which compels us to retreat from engaging in any kind of debate, civil or otherwise. Instead, we vilify our ideological opponents as justification for our unwillingness to consider their opinions.

This raises yet another ethical question: Is it better to speak out on hot-button issues, knowing that the likely effect will be to alienate large swaths of the populace; or is it better to simply avoid those topics and attempt to civilize the conversation first, in hope of creating a society of greater forbearance where more substantive topics can be raised and thoughtfully examined?

The absence of overly controversial topics should make my own conclusion clear. However, I did risk flirting with a few of those issues along the way, especially in the last section.

Only when we are able and willing to work through our most prickly problems will we have a real chance of solving them. My hope is that this book will contribute to moving the conversation in a more rational direction.

In 2003, MSNBC news anchor Brian Williams was attached to a convoy of Chinook helicopters in Iraq when a sandstorm forced the mission to abort. Once on the ground, word came that a different helicopter in the convoy had almost been shot down by a rocket-propelled grenade.

Then the story began to change. In one version, Mr. Williams seemed to imply having witnessed the attack on the lead helicopter himself. In another, the grenade tore a hole in his helicopter but failed to detonate.

By 2013, he claimed to have feared for his life when his own chopper came under fire.

Then, in 2015, Brian Williams recounted how his helicopter had actually been shot down by an RPG, and how his team was rescued by the American 3rd Infantry.

Five days later, Mr. Williams went back on the air to apologize for his flight of fantasy.

Personally, I don't believe that Brian Williams ever set out to deliberately distort the truth. It seems more likely that he just tweaked the narrative here and there to make it a little more dramatic. But after a dozen years of embellishment, the story of his chopper ride had turned into a work of fiction. Almost overnight, he went from being one of television's most respected journalists to being a punchline.

Haven't we all done the same thing—embellished the details of a moderately interesting story to make it more compelling? Aren't some of our favorite movies "based on a true story" or, even more disingenuously, "inspired by true events"? Those small-print disclaimers may preempt charges of misrepresentation. But what is the far-reaching effect on our respect for the truth when the truth isn't good enough to hold our interest?

This is the natural consequence of living in an age when anything has to be sensational if it's going to get noticed at all. Exaggeration is really no different from lying. Truth doesn't need our help to make it better. And if we blur the lines between reality and fakery even a little, soon we'll forget that there are any lines at all.

It's the blurring of lines that's so dangerous. By relentlessly and insidiously expanding the gray areas of our lives, we begin to believe that there are no hard boundaries, that nothing is black and white. And once everything is negotiable, why should we search for absolutes? If every path is equally acceptable, why agonize over choosing this one or that? If everything is gray, why should we grapple to differentiate between one shade and another?

This is what King Solomon meant when he declared: *Do not remove the boundaries of eternity, which were set in place by your fathers.*

My mother told me that as a student at UC Berkeley in the 1950s (before the hippie revolution), whenever she and her friends went out on the town in San Francisco, she dressed in a suit, heels, hat, and gloves. San Francisco was "the city," the cosmopolitan center of the west coast. One simply did not step onto its streets wearing anything other than one's finest.

Those days are long gone, and not entirely for the better. Consider the underlying message of expectations, standards, and respect. Consider the impact even one person's code of personal conduct has on the surrounding culture. This is the essence of *civility* which, observes Professor Stephen L. Carter, is the root of *civilization*.

Of course, moral sensitivities change over generations. But if we allow our core principles to erode, no matter how gradually, we eventually find ourselves untethered to any absolute boundaries of right and wrong, drifting inexorably toward the edge of the map, where there be monsters—the unslayable dragons of self-interest, self-indulgence, and self-righteousness that prey on even the most well-intentioned navigators who cross the seas of ethical conflict and deliberation.

The more unethical the society around us becomes, the more challenging it is for any of us to maintain our own standards of integrity. How can we expect a promising young athlete to refrain from using steroids when he can't compete honestly with others who flout the rules? How can we expect a young journalist to exercise journalistic restraint when she can't compete with sensationalism that replaces principled reportage? How can we expect our politicians to demonstrate authentic statesmanship when they need to negotiate a system of corruption and rampant partisanship to gain and hold public office? How can we expect young executives to see themselves as team players when those above them have attained their positions by stepping on colleagues in their climb toward the top?

Eventually, when the foundational rules that govern civil society have become forgotten, what hope is there for society to survive?

That's why it's critical to carefully consider the words we say and how we say them. That's why it's crucial how others see us and how we see ourselves. We need to accommodate the needs and expectations of those around us; but we have to balance that accommodation against our own needs and aspirations. We are simultaneously individuals *and* members of a society; our success balancing the perpetual tension between the two is what determines the measure of our ethical identity.

At the risk of trying to appear clever, I would like to propose that we view *ETHICS* as an acronym for six essential character traits that, collectively, produce an ethical mindset.

Empathy. What all four models of moral conduct have in common is a sensitivity for how individual actions affect the world we live in. Before we can begin to consider ourselves ethical, we need to feel the joy and pain, the hope and fear, the wants and dreams of our fellow human beings.

Trustworthiness. If we aren't honest in both our speech and personal conduct, if we don't comport ourselves with integrity, we will never earn the trust of those around us. Without trust, no relationship can flourish, and no community can survive.

Humility. According to scripture, Moses was both the greatest prophet of all times and the most humble man who ever lived. How can both be true? Because humility does not require us to deny our talents or successes. Rather, it requires us to see them as *gifts*, an outlook that fills us with a sense of duty, purpose, and moral responsibility.

Inquisitiveness. We should never allow ourselves to think that we know enough, that we understand enough, that we are wise enough. Seeking knowledge and understanding requires a mindset of curiosity and constant improvement. No matter how much we attain or accomplish, we can always be and do better.

Courage. It's scary to do the right thing, to risk rebuke or even open hostility for holding others to account, for taking a stand against what's expected or what's popular. But as we learn from Edmund Burke: Evil flourishes when good people do nothing. And, as we learn from Hillel: If not now, when?

Self-discipline. Am I doing the hard work required to set standards for myself and strive to live up to them? Nothing worthwhile comes without determined effort, and building good character is foundational to building a strong business. We can't expect others to set the bar higher than we are willing to set it for ourselves.

During the question and answer session following an ethics keynote, an attendee posed this hypothetical: While shopping in a department store, you witness a counter worker being verbally abused by a superior. Should you intervene?

I responded that every situation is different and that, as we have already observed, there is no quick-reference guide for making ethical decisions. The best we can do is cultivate ethical sensitivity so we are prepared to respond to situations as best we can.

That is all true, but after the fact I felt I had not served my questioner as well as I might have. No matter how abstract the scenario, ethics demands that we reject the false premise of a binary choice—either I confront the superior or I do nothing. Acting ethically often calls for a measure of creativity.

True story: Walking back to her car through a grocery store parking lot, a woman found her attention drawn to two high-end cars parked side by side facing opposite directions. Across the short space between their open windows, a man and a woman were shouting furiously at one another. In the back seat of one car, a girl of 7 or 8 years sat statue-like, as each of her obviously divorced parents insisted that it was the other's turn to look after the daughter.

As the onlooker debated whether she should or could intervene, she spotted a police car nearby. She strode over and hastily explained the situation to the officer, who approached the ex-couple and told them they were illegally stopped and needed to move on.

Sometimes our own inability to make things better can leave us heartbroken. We may not be able to address the root problem, but we can still look for a way to interrupt an escalating situation enough to make things better—at least for a little while. Even the smallest intervention reminds us that we do not have to accept the role of helpless bystanders.

Let's go back to our counter worker and her supervisor. Maybe she really does deserve rebuke. But does it have to be in front of the customers? Does she deserve to be publicly humiliated? We can certainly empathize with her distress and feel her desperate hope that someone will rescue her from her plight.

Imagine that you approach the counter with one of the following lines:

"Excuse me, I'm having trouble finding something in my size. Could I have assistance please?"

"Sorry to interrupt, but this young lady was extremely helpful when I came in yesterday and I didn't have a chance to thank her properly."

"Do you have a moment? I'm writing a magazine article on workplace conflict. Could I ask you a few questions, please?"

Is it dishonest to misrepresent yourself to spare a stranger unnecessary pain? That itself is part of the ethical equation. But an impromptu cocktail of caring, courage, and creativity will likely leave everyone feeling better. At least it will short-circuit an ugly exchange. At best, it will hit the reset button and turn events in a more palatable direction.

Ethics is not a code of compliance or a book of rules. Ethics is a mindset that emerges naturally from the awareness that all our actions matter, that the *noblesse oblige* of being human requires us to conduct ourselves with thoughtfulness, with decorum, with dignity, with courage, and with self-restraint. By acting ethically, we contribute to the creation of a better society and a better world. When we live in a better world, we can't help but become better ourselves.

When we act ethically, those around us notice. When we do so repeatedly and consistently, we earn the admiration and respect of others, which inspires them to emulate us. Once that happens, then we will find ourselves on our way to restoring a truly civil society in which all of us, together, work to seek common ground, to solve our common problems, and to forge a community in which our differences are not cause for acrimony but the source of our greatest strength, our most profound pleasure, and our most enduring success.

Acknowledgments

Books are more mysterious than babies. After all, we know where babies come from, and we have a general idea how they are going to develop.

A book often springs into existence as if from nowhere and grows in unpredictable directions. That was certainly the case with this one. As I sat over coffee with my friend and mentor Steve Epner, I articulated—as I have many times—my vision of ethics as the challenging business of seeking clarity in the gray areas between what is legal and illegal.

On this occasion, however, the words tumbled out of my mouth in a new combination. "Ethics," I said, "is about grappling with the gray."

Steve's face lit up: "That's a book title!" he exclaimed.

And so it came to pass that the handful of ethical scenarios I had collected for my keynote presentations formed the nucleus of the work you have just completed reading.

Thank you, Steve, for your inspiration, your guidance, and your friendship.

Since embarking on my new career as an ethics speaker, I've discovered a second family—the colleagues and mentors among the membership of the National Speakers Association. At the risk of omitting someone worthy of mention, I'm compelled to acknowledge those who influenced and supported me from the start, as well as those who invested their time and thought in this particular project: Lois Creamer, Tony Ruesing, Lisa Yakobi, Wayne Schoeneberg, Sam Silverstein, Patricia Fripp, and Bob Burg. Thanks also to David Horsager and Dan Thurmon, whose inspiration and encouragement have ever prodded me forward.

Thanks to Syd Chase, Rabbi Doniel Grunewald, and Dave Bricker for their editorial counsel, and to Rabbi Simcha Weinberg for his sometimes mystifying enthusiasm. Thank you to Rabbi Yitzchok Zilberstein, whose anthology *Ha'arev Noh* and its English adaptation *What If…* provided several of the scenarios I address through the lens of ethics.

Thanks to my rabbis and teachers who trained me to apply the ancient wisdom of the Talmud to complexities of the modern world: Rabbi Osher

Reich, Rabbi Dovid Gottleib, Rabbi Shmuel Geller, Rabbi Shabsy Black, and Rabbi Nota Schiller, as well as Rabbi Mendel Weinbach, Rabbi Ephraim Oratz, and Rabbi Nachman Bulman, of blessed memory.

Thanks to Nigel Wyatt for making the introduction to Business Expert Press, and to Rob Zwettler David Wasieleski, and the BEP editorial and production team.

My children, Avigayil, Yaakov, Yitzy, and Devorah, inspire me daily to leave behind as much of myself as possible. My mother, who takes a mother's pleasure in every milestone, guarantees that I always have at least one avid fan.

Thank you to my wife, Sara Miriam, who has supported me through more unexpected twists and turns than we ever expected when we began our journey together 32 years ago.

And finally, thank you to the One who gives wisdom, for leading me back to the traditions and teaching of my people and endowing me with the ability to articulate the eternal wisdom handed down from Sinai, which forms the foundation upon which the most noble pursuits of mankind have been erected.

May we all find inspiration to be good and do good, to be inspired and inspire others to walk in the ways of virtue together.

Recommended Readings

Badaracco, J.L. 1997. *Defining Moments*. Boston: Harvard Business School Press.
Integrity by Stephen L. Carter.
The Righteous Mind by Jonathan Haidt.
Predictably Irrational by Dan Ariely.
Give and Take by Adam Grant.

About the Author

Yonason Goldson is director of Ethical Imperatives, LLC, teaching professionals how good ethics is good business and the benefits of intellectual diversity. He's a keynote speaker, TEDx presenter, and community rabbi, as well as a repentant hitchhiker, recovered circumnavigator, former newspaper columnist, and retired high school teacher in St. Louis, where he and his wife live happily as empty nesters.

Visit his website at yonasongoldson.com.

Also by Yonason Goldson
Fix Your Broken Windows
Proverbial Beauty
Dawn to Destiny
A Crucible for Silver
Celestial Navigation

Index

Acronym, ethics, 152–153
Age of Acrimony, xxi–xxxii
Ambiguity, xxii

Book of Proverbs (King Solomon), xv
Business mindset, 25–61

Carter, Stephen L., 145, 151, xxix
Civility, 151, xxiv
Company culture, 132–133, xxviii
Compliance, 92, 154, xxiv, xxix
Corporate culture, 90
Courage, 152–153
COVID-19 pandemic, xiii

Defining Moments (Joseph Badaracco, Jr.,), xvi
Delta Airlines, 131

Empathy, 32, 147, 152, xxvi
Ethical actions steps, xxxi–xxxii
Ethical business, 25–61
  case studies
    "A Drop in the Cup," 39–41
    "Checking Out," 37–38
    "Commuting Sentences," 58–59
    "Happy Birth-day," 35–36
    "Invisible Customers," 50–51
    "It's All About You," 56–57
    "It's all in Your Mind," 27–28
    "Lights Out," 32–34
    "Many Happy Returns," 44–45
    "No One Here but Us Chickens," 52–55
    "On the Wing," 29–31
    "Say Cheese," 46–47
    "State of Mind," 42–43
    "Strolling Along," 60–61
    "Two-Faced," 48–49
Ethical education, 63–77
  case studies
    "Chilling Effects," 67–69

"Everyone Is above Average," 65–66
"The Grand Design," 70–72
"The Other Foot," 73–75
"Yearning to Be Free," 76–77
Ethical headlines, 129–146
  case studies
    "All for One?," 131–133
    "Crying Wolf?," 136–138
    "In or Out?," 134–135
    "Paved with Good Intentions," 141–143
    "Standing on Principle?," 139–140
    "Whistleblowing in the Dark?," 144–146
Ethical leadership, 112, xxviii
Ethical mindset, 43, 149, 154, xvi, xxix, xxvii
Ethical relationship
  case studies
    "A Bump in the Night," 9–10
    "Be Our Guest," 5–6
    "Bliss is Ignorance," 21–23
    "It's a Sure Bet," 15–17
    "Living on the Edge," 11–12
    "No Cancellations," 18–20
    "The Gift of Acceptance," 7–8
    "The Ugly Truth," 3–4
    "Who Gets the Bill," 13–14
Ethical society, 79–128
  case studies
    "Behind Drawer #1," 81–82
    "Boxing for Dollars," 101–102
    "By the Book?," 85–87
    "Dressed to Distress," 93–95
    "Eye-to-I," 118–119
    "Gold diggers," 113–114
    "In the Bag," 103–105
    "Leap of Faith?," 115–117
    "On Thin Ice," 123–125
    "Pay as You Go," 96–97

Ethical society (*continued*)
 "Seeds of Doubt ," 88–90
 "Share the Wealth," 83–84
 "Snake Eyes," 111–112
 "The Coin of the Realm," 91–92
 "Unimpeachable Logic?," 98–100
 "Unsafe at Any Speed ," 106–110
 "Virtual Dominoes," 120–122
 "Why Vote?," 126–128
Ethics
 acronym for, 184–153
 defined, xi
 description of, xxv
 legislation of, xxiv–xxvii
 principles of, xxii–xxx
Ethics of Fathers, 1, 63, 129, xxix, xxx

Feingold, Russ, 141
Foot, Philippa, 108
Frozen, 67

Good Samaritan laws, 33

Humility, 152

Inquisitiveness, 152
Integrity, 28, 97, 104
 character and, xxv
 electoral, 141
 informational, evaluation of, xxxi
 intellectual, xxii–xxiv, xxxii
Intuitionism, xiv

Kantianism, xiv
Kennedy, John F., 94
King David, xvii
Koehler., D.J., 148

Leadership, 112
Leadership mindset, 90, 112, xxix
McCain, John, 141
McDonald, 40
Mindset
 ethical, 43, 149, 154, xvi, xxix, xxvii
 ethics and, 154, xxvii
Morality
 defined, xiv
 description of, xxv
Moral vision, 147
Moynihan, Daniel Patrick, xxi

Rabbi Safra, 27
Rationalism, xxi–xxxii

Self-discipline, 152
Shin Dong-hyuk, 147
Snowden, Eric, 141
Spielberg, Steven, 123

Tainter, Joseph, 120
The Oxford Companion to Philosophy, xii
Trump, Donald, 139
Trustworthiness, 152

United Airlines, 29, 93
Utilitarianism, xiii

Virtue ethics, xiv–xv

Whistleblowing, 144

Yates, Simon, 11

Zilberstein, Y., 61

OTHER TITLES IN OUR BUSINESS ETHICS AND CORPORATE CITIZENSHIP COLLECTION

David M. Wasieleski, *Editor*

- *Business and the Culture of Ethics* by Quentin Langley
- *Corporate Citizenship and Sustainability: Measuring Intangible, Fiscal, and Ethical Assets* by Jayaraman Rajah Iyer
- *Applied Humanism: How to Create More Effective and Ethical Businesses* by Jennifer Hancock
- *Powerful Performance: How to Be Influential, Ethical, and Successful in Business* by Mark Eyre
- *Ethics In The Legal Sector* by Carolyn Plump
- *Leadership Matters? Finding Voice, Connection and Meaning in the 21st Century* by Christopher Mabey and David Knights
- *Educating Business Professionals: The Call Beyond Competence and Expertise* by Lana S. Nino and Susan D. Gotsch
- *Adapting to Change: The Business of Climate Resilience* by Ann Goodman
- *Social Media Ethics Made Easy: How to Comply with FTC Guidelines* by Joseph W. Barnes
- *Business Ethics: A Moral Reasoning Framework* by Annabel Beerel
- *War Stories: Fighting, Competing, Imagining, Leading* by Leigh Hafrey
- *Leadership Ethics: Moral Power for Business Leaders* by Lindsay Thompson
- *Shaping the Future of Work: What Future Worker, Business, Government, and Education Leaders Need To Do For All To Prosper* by Thomas A. Kochan
- *Working Ethically in Finance: Clarifying Our Vocation* by Anthony Asher
- *Sales Ethics: How To Sell Effectively While Doing the Right Thing* by Alberto Aleo and Alice Alessandri

Concise and Applied Business Books

The Collection listed above is one of 30 business subject collections that Business Expert Press has grown to make BEP a premiere publisher of print and digital books. Our concise and applied books are for...

- Professionals and Practitioners
- Faculty who adopt our books for courses
- Librarians who know that BEP's Digital Libraries are a unique way to offer students ebooks to download, not restricted with any digital rights management
- Executive Training Course Leaders
- Business Seminar Organizers

Business Expert Press books are for anyone who needs to dig deeper on business ideas, goals, and solutions to everyday problems. Whether one print book, one ebook, or buying a digital library of 110 ebooks, we remain the affordable and smart way to be business smart. For more information, please visit **www.businessexpertpress.com**, or contact **sales@businessexpertpress.com**.

CPSIA information can be obtained
at www.ICGtesting.com
Printed in the USA
BVHW091629221120
593764BV00005B/12